THE WADDINGTONS STORY

FROM THE EARLY DAYS TO MONOPOLY, THE MAXWELL BIDS AND INTO THE NEXT MILLENNIUM

VICTOR WATSON

NORTHERN HERITAGE
PUBLICATIONS

Published by Northern Heritage Publications
an imprint of Jeremy Mills Publishing Limited
www.jeremymillspublishing.co.uk

First published 2008
Text and images © Victor Watson

The moral right of Victor Watson to be indentified as the author of this work has been asserted. All rights reserved. No part of this book may be reproduced in any form or by any means without prior permission in writing from the publisher.

ISBN: 978-1-906600-36-5 (paperback)
       978-1-906600-38-9 (hardback)

Printed and bound in the UK
by Riley Dunn & Wilson Ltd.
www.rdwdigital.co.uk
+44 (0)1484 534323

Front cover image:
Victor Watson peering through the printed playing cards.

CONTENTS

ACKNOWLEDGEMENTS		V
FOREWORD		VII
PREFACE		IX
CHAPTER ONE	Victor Watson – A Self-Made Man	1
CHAPTER TWO	A History of Waddingtons: Written by Douglas Brearley in 1973 (H. D. (Doug) Brearley was a lifetime employee of Waddingtons who became a director and was one of the most knowledgeable and dedicated members of the team.)	7
CHAPTER THREE	Victor Watson's Own Account (Taken from the *Waddington Team* Magazines of 1927 and 1928)	37
CHAPTER FOUR	A Reminiscence of the Early Days (By Victor Watson, written in 1928)	57
CHAPTER FIVE	A Grandson's Recollections	63
CHAPTER SIX	Lithography and Colour Separation	73
CHAPTER SEVEN	Enter the Game Monopoly	77
CHAPTER EIGHT	Playing Cards and De La Rue	89
CHAPTER NINE	Another Acorn, Another Tall Oak: From Satona to Plastic Containers	95

CHAPTER TEN	The Bid of 1967	97
CHAPTER ELEVEN	The Bids of Norton and Wright and Maxwell in 1983	103
CHAPTER TWELVE	Maxwell's Bid of 1984	137
CHAPTER THIRTEEN	The Maxwell Bids – The Lighter Side	149
CHAPTER FOURTEEN	What Became of Waddingtons?	153
APPENDICES		165
INDEX		187
ABOUT THE AUTHOR		208

ACKNOWLEDGEMENTS

I AM ESPECIALLY grateful to Ann Hills for typing many drafts and redrafts of the manuscript; she can read my writing better than I can.

My thanks for checking and advising go to my brother John Watson, to David Perry, Peter Stephens and Martin Young. Ranny Barton and Phil Orbanes corrected the chapter on Monopoly. I am indebted to my editor, Natasha Roberts.

Last but not least, I thank Robert McClements, who encouraged me to publish when I felt that the book would only interest those who had been involved, and those who will peruse the index!

FOREWORD

VICTOR WATSON IS an extraordinary man whose generosity of time and wisdom has touched all who know him. His achievements are myriad and his contribution to industry, good causes and individuals are set out in the biographical notes at the end of this book.

I am privileged to have worked with him over the years and I am enormously grateful for his advice and encouragement. When I was asked to help establish PrintYorkshire in 2005 my first action was to phone Victor and ask him two things: firstly, did he think the initiative was appropriate and secondly, if he did, would he consider becoming its founding President. His immediate reply was, 'Yes, to both'. That seemed a good omen. Over the last three years the printing industry in the Yorkshire and Humber region has bucked the national trend – in spite of the reduction in the number of companies from 1500 to 1260, employment has stayed at around 20,000 and the gross income has risen from £1.5 billion to £1.85 billion.

Some readers will know some of the story of Waddingtons – it epitomises the 'cluster' company that Michael Porter, Harvard business guru, describes and which prompted Yorkshire Forward, the region's development agency, to work with the BPIF (British Printing Industry Federation) to support the industry. Some readers will know part of Victor's wider achievements. To see them all together is to see a piece of history and the personal dimension which completes the picture.

With thanks,

Roberts McClements
Chief Executive, PrintYorkshire

(March 2008)

PREFACE

THIS BOOK COVERS about eighty years of the existence of John Waddington Ltd (latterly Waddington plc). It is not an exhaustive history of the company. My view is that company histories are largely unread. I have a bookcase full of them and I cannot claim to have read more than a few from beginning to end, although I have perused the indexes! Instead, I have focused on a few of the most important periods and developments in the life of the company, and the people who featured at these times.

The first part of this work deals with the extraordinary achievement of my grandfather and his son, who was my father. My grandfather was appointed manager in 1913, and by 1938 Waddingtons was transformed from a small jobbing printer in dire straits to one of the largest printing companies in the land, and a household name to boot. The next section recalls the further development of the company during and after the Second World War and the products and technologies it used, and includes my own first-hand recollections of the game of Monopoly and its role in the fortunes of Waddingtons. The book then goes on to describe the four hostile takeover bids which assailed Waddingtons, starting with that of Mardon in 1967 and then progressing to the bids of Norton and Wright and Robert Maxwell and the British Printing Corporation in 1983 and 1984.

Finally, I have dealt with the frequent question of 'what became of Waddingtons'. If, dear reader, you are a pessimist, you will find the story very sad. You may recall the words of Winston Churchill; 'A country that forgets its past has no future', and apply that aphorism to the Waddingtons of about fifteen years ago. If, however, you are an optimist, you will accept that as some organisms die, others thrive. It is how the natural world works, and the laws which govern animals apply also to business. Waddingtons became Communisis, and while it was not a metamorphosis, there is a thread which still links Communisis and Waddingtons. As the new business thrives, it makes me optimistic for the future of businesses in general and the printing trade in particular.

CHAPTER ONE

VICTOR WATSON – A SELF-MADE MAN

My grandfather, Victor Hugo Watson, was a remarkable man who, at the age of thirty-five, was appointed manager of a small bankrupt printing business, which he turned into a large, successful company, and a household name in Britain. The company was John Waddington Ltd. The place was Leeds in Yorkshire.

Victor Watson was born in 1878 in Brixton near to the famous cricket ground, the Oval. As he was born within the 'sound of Bow Bells' he could claim to be a true Cockney, but in mature life he was an ardent Yorkshireman, especially where cricket was concerned. His father was Thomas Watson, a commercial traveller and a part-time professional singer; one story is that he sold prints for a Bradford company. Thomas knew many people in the theatre world, which may have explained the choice of the literary name of 'Victor Hugo' for his son.

When Victor was very young the family moved to Leeds. This was a return to Yorkshire for them because Thomas' father had come from Glasgow to work as a coal miner at Thornhill, near Dewsbury. Then, because Thomas was still a boy at the time of his father's death, he was brought up by the Peace family, who ran the Scarborough Inn at Thornhill. Thomas went on to marry Elizabeth Peace, and it was a relation of hers who married Thomas' daughter Kate and persuaded Victor to join Waddingtons in 1908. Victor left school at twelve to be a butcher's boy. Those who knew him described him as high spirited and energetic. He may have left school at a very young age, but the family had books at home and there were relatives who encouraged his reading and improvement. Cricket was also a major activity in his life, both in the street and on the field at Burley Park in Leeds, which was the team he joined as a junior.

My father, Norman Watson, told me that Victor had become a butcher's boy while Thomas was away, and upon his return Thomas did not rest until he got Victor apprenticed to a well-respected firm of printers, Goodall and Suddick. The indentures read as follows:

> This indenture witnesseth that Victor Hugo Watson of 20 Fenton Place in the City of Leeds a lithographer by and with the consent of his father Thomas Watson of the same place, Commercial Traveller doth put himself apprentice to George Austin Suddick of Leeds and Bradford both in the County of York Lithographer Stationer and Bookbinder trading under the style or firm of Goodall and Suddick and hereinafter referred to as the said Master to learning his Art and with him after the Manner of an Apprentice to serve from the Nineteenth day of January One thousand eight hundred and ninety four unto the full End and Term of five years.
>
> Victor Hugo Watson
Thomas Watson
George Austin Suddick
>
> ....put their Hands and Seals the twentieth day of February and in the fifty seventh year of the Reign of our Sovereign Lady Queen Victoria by the Grace of God of the United Kingdom of Great Britain and Ireland Queen Defender of the Faith and the year of our Lord One Thousand Eight Hundred and Ninety Four.

It is difficult for us in 2008 to imagine life as it was in the late nineteenth century. Of the children of Thomas and Elizabeth Watson, five out of the first six died before they were seventeen years old. Only Hannah lived beyond her teenage years and she died in Northern Ireland at the age of thirty-three. She was a nanny, and I am told that she died of a snake bite (her grave is at Tullyaughnish near to Rathmelton). The seventh child, Kate, was born in 1877, and lived until 1959. Next came Victor, who lived until 1943. I can remember Kate and Victor's younger siblings Elia, Tom, Claude, Vernon and Horace (especially Claude and Horace, who were great fun). Horace was with his father when Thomas died in Duncan Street in Leeds. Horace was seven at the time and Victor was twenty-two and, I think, just married. He and Ethel (née Dawson) brought up Horace as if he was their son. Certainly Horace always thought of my father, Norman, as a younger brother.

Times were hard but not desperate, as can be seen in this transcript of a story my father told to me towards the end of his life.

NORMAN WATSON'S ACCOUNT AS RELATED TO VICTOR, HIS SON

6 January 1967

Year approximately 1911 – Norman, aged 8

The family in those days lived in Ebor Place near to Woodhouse Moor. It was my maternal grandmother, Elizabeth Dawson, who taught the family how to live well on a very low income. She used to send young Norman down to the Refinery in Park Cross Street for two stones of rind, and when he returned she would render it down and have enough dripping for a month. If a man went to work on dripping and bread he was well set up for the day.

She used to work as a cleaner at the Town Hall and it was her job to clean out the Chief Constable's office. She had to be there at six o'clock and would usually catch a tram, but on very icy days the trams were not allowed to run down Belle Vue Road, so she would set off at five o'clock in the morning to walk.

On one fateful day she was asked by her daughter, Ethel, to call at Dr Roberts and ask him to call and look at Victor, who was quite ill. There was no health service in those days but Victor Watson paid 1/- a week to the Doctor for service when he needed it – the Doctor's own insurance scheme. Ethel and her friend, Mary Illingworth, were up very early cleaning the house so that it was sparkling fresh for the arrival of the Doctor. She put on her best frock, and her young son Norman who was kept back from school for examination waited at the window. At quarter to nine the Doctor arrived in a very smart wagonette with two fine horses, and what a splendid figure he made as he alighted, dressed in a black coat, striped trousers, spats and silk topper. He looked the responsible and educated citizen that he was. Before he reached the door it was opened for him to enter.

He asked Ethel Watson how she was, and if she had managed to overcome the problem of breast feeding her latest baby, Eric. Then they went upstairs and he soon confirmed that Victor had indeed got scarlet *fever. He examined Norman and young Muriel and said that he had better call every day for four days to examine the whole family. He then said that the fever wagon would call to take Mr Watson to Killingbeck Hospital at three o'clock. He gave Ethel Watson a list of the clothes that would be needed and recommended that her husband should be dressed in really warm clothing for the journey. 'You can always take up a good suit for him, later on', he said. At three o'clock the fever wagon arrived but Victor Watson was not dressed in his oldest and warmest clothes; he would have none of that. He put on his best suit for the occasion and all the street turned out to witness this exciting event.*

The Matron at Killingbeck was very relieved when Victor Watson finally recovered, for he disturbed the peace of the hospital on several occasions. The most notable was the mock marriage arranged between one of the patients and one of the nurses with all the children acting as choristers, bridesmaids and pageboys, and then came the day when the few men who were in hospital decided that the flowers should be watered. They took the fire hose through the children's ward; Victor, of course, was at the business end. One of his friends turned on the hydrant and to everyone's surprise very little water reached the nozzle; most of it seeped through holes in the perished pipe. The children's ward was drenched, with bedding completely soaked and the whole floor swimming with water before it was realised what was happening and the hydrant turned off. The threats of the Matron were soon eliminated by Victor Watson's claim that he would tell his friend the Deputy Lord Mayor of the state in which the hospital's fire equipment was kept.

Thus, we have a glimpse of how they lived. But where did they live? I have done my best to find out. From Victor Watson's indentures (1894) we know that his home then was 20 Fenton Place, Leeds. Nowadays the Jubilee Wing of Leeds General Infirmary stands where Fenton Place once was. I believe that Victor married Ethel between 1900 and 1902, and they lived at 5 Belle Vue Place where Norman was born. Belle Vue Road is still there, running from the west side of the old Leeds Grammar School down to Park Lane, but Belle Vue Place is now the site of a block of flats.

Subsequently the family lived at 26 Ashville Terrace, which was the house at the end of the row next to the railway line. From there they moved up the hill to Ebor Place, taking up residence in one of the end houses next to the inaptly named Royal Park Road. Both Ashville Terrace and Ebor Place are still there, but they are very run down. If you start at Burley Road and go up

Cardigan Road you pass the old factory of Harrison Townsend, where Victor worked as a lithographer. (It was called Cardigan Press until after the Second World War, when it was bought by Waddingtons and became RustCraft, a greetings card company jointly owned with RustCraft of Canada). Further up the road on the left, just before Burley Park railway station, is Ashville Terrace. It is less than half a mile from Headingley cricket ground. Before you reach Ashville Terrace you come to Royal Park Road which leads up the hill to Woodhouse Moor, near to where the old Victoria cricket ground used to be. Ebor Place is just beyond the old Royal Park Primary School, with its different entrances etched in stone: 'GIRLS' at one end and 'BOYS' at the other. I would guess that Victor and Ethel's children probably went there because it was a very short walk. Norman then went to the Leeds Grammar School, which was less than half a mile away. The area is now decrepit, but there is a park at the top of the hill and Burley Park is near the bottom. With very few cars in those days, and friendly neighbours all of the same background, it must have been a pleasant place to live. The whole area is peppered with placenames which incorporate 'Cardigan' and 'Brudenell'. Many people are unaware that the Brudenell family owned much of the land there. James Brudenell, Earl of Cardigan, was the man who led the Charge of the Light Brigade into the 'Valley of Death' at Balaclava in 1854. He also wore a knitted woollen ganzie which became known as a 'cardigan'.

It was just over a mile to the centre of Leeds from Ebor Place, and the next move across Woodhouse Moor took the family only a little further out of town. At the time of Victor's promotion to become the manager of John Waddingtons Ltd, they moved to a grand house, 3 Woodhouse Cliff, with countryside beyond and probably a little less of the awful smoke of Leeds. They lived next to Dr Dunlop who I remember well, along with his son John, as they were both members of Moortown Golf Club.

After Norman and Ruby (née Hawker) had married, Victor and Ethel moved to Clare House, Scotland Lane, Horsforth, which is still there, although I'm not so sure about the monkey puzzle tree which stood in the garden. Like many middle-class Victorian houses Clare House had four main downstairs rooms: a kitchen and dining room at the back, and two front rooms. One of these was the drawing room with its grand piano. The other was the billiard room where we boys spent many happy hours, often playing with the maid, Agnes Kavanagh, who became very good at snooker. Agnes was Irish, young and high spirited. She lived in, and did all sorts in addition to housework. She caddied for Grandad at Horsforth Golf Club and on one famous occasion at the encouragement of Grandad's partners, had a go at the seventeenth at Horsforth, where she hit a great drive and was down in four; it was the talk of the Club for ages! She played every game with us and this was condoned by Granny and Grandad. Grandad himself would play cricket with us on the lawn, but I remember him best for bridge, solo and hearts at the card table, and especially for chess. 'All great generals play chess', I heard him say more than once. 'The game teaches you to look ahead, to try to determine the strategy of your opponent and above all develop a strategy of your own.' He played tennis at the factory on the asphalt court behind the canteen, usually with his secretary (my mother-to-be) and her colleagues, and one or other of the managers; it was a popular lunchtime pastime and the games occasionally went on so long that they had to work late to make up time.

To round off this short introduction I should mention cricket in more detail. Victor was a keen member of the Headingley Cricket Club, which played on the Clarendon Ground just off Cardigan Road. This was not the Headingley Ground where Yorkshire County Cricket Club played their first game in 1891, having played in Sheffield, Holbeck (Leeds) and Hunslet (Leeds) until then. Victor was on the committee of Headingley Cricket Club in 1914, and in 1921 they made a presentation to him; it was an illuminated book which I treasure to this day.

CHAPTER TWO

A HISTORY OF WADDINGTONS

WRITTEN BY DOUGLAS BREARLEY IN 1973

IT IS INEVITABLE that historical records should commence in a vague way. It would be surprising if this was not so because small events lead to greater ones and are often unnoticed and treated as unimportant. This position is exactly the same as far as the first records of John Waddington Ltd are concerned and the early days would be shrouded in mystery but for the fortunate fact that some of the happenings were put in writing by the first Victor Watson.

John Waddington was a tall man of impressive appearance who wore the type of cavalry moustache which was the fashion in the late Victorian and early Edwardian days. He was an apprenticed printer but it seems reasonable to suppose that he would have fared better in the theatrical world rather than printing for the theatre business. John Waddington started a printing business before the present century by entering into partnership with Wilson Barrett, who was an actor manager at the Leeds Grand Theatre. A company was formed under the name of Waddingtons Ltd for printing theatre posters and other printed matter needed for advertising stage productions. The premises were opened in Camp Road, Leeds, on the north side of the river, not far from the present University. The company must have been operating before 1900 as it is on record that a George Mitchell was apprenticed with Waddingtons Ltd in 1898 and there is available in an old copy of the *Yorkshire Harlequin*, a theatrical publication dated 5 January 1898, an advertisement describing Waddingtons Ltd as colour printers.

It appears that John Waddington was a very difficult character and the partnership with Wilson Barrett did not last, as very soon after the company was formed there was a breach between them which led to John Waddington leaving the business and starting one of his own. Waddingtons Ltd continued operating in Camp Road and John Waddington himself obtained some premises in Great Wilson Street which was south of the river and nearer the growing industrial part of Leeds in the direction of Hunslet. John Waddington's new business very soon ran into money difficulties and was rescued by Frederick Eley, the bank manager of the local National Provincial Bank, where John Waddington placed his account.

Mr Eley suggested the formation of a private limited company which was created on the 31 January 1905 and named John Waddington Ltd. The first directors were H. M. Carter, a company promoter and John Waddington, and after a short period they were joined by a William Peacock. Within two years this Board was strengthened by the addition of Edgar Lupton, a member of a well known Leeds family, who was immediately appointed chairman. It is interesting to note that two of the early shareholders were John Martin Harvey and Fred Karno, and although there is a humorous twist concerning the second name, it demonstrates how closely the business was connected with the theatrical world.

In August 1908, William Peacock resigned and Ralph B. Stephens, a stockbroker in the Leeds area,[1] took his place and became financial director and during the same year Arthur Copson Peake, a Leeds solicitor, who later became Sir Arthur Copson Peake, joined the Board. John Waddington pressed the other directors for money to buy lithographic machinery in spite of the fact that it was said that John Waddington Ltd had the finest collection of wooden type in the country, this type being used for letterpress printing. The business was occupying the second floor of the building in Great Wilson Street and to house the lithographic machinery, the bottom floor of the same building was rented. Prior to this arrangement any lithographic work needed was given to other printers, but now that the lithographic printing was carried out within the company, more staff were needed. Victor Watson, then a lithographer at Harrison Townsend, was invited to join John Waddington Ltd as lithographic foreman. Victor Watson was a dynamic character and although when he first joined the company he faced great opposition from the people already in the business, his personality and energy smoothed out all problems. He improved the quality of the printing and went far beyond his duties by obtaining additional orders which

---

1 *Note by Victor Watson:* Peter Stephens, the nephew of R. B. Stephens, thinks that R. B. Stephens may have been employed by Frederich Eley at the National Provincial Bank at this time, and only became a stockbroker later on.

very soon increased the turnover by 33.3%. This rapid improvement was dissipated by the peculiar business methods of John Waddington which included the accumulation of many bad debts which were never written off. Money difficulties became more and more severe and it became apparent that something had to happen and finally on the 7 March 1913 John Waddington resigned. The directors were about to close the business down but were persuaded by Victor Watson to allow trading to proceed for a further period. He was appointed manager and a month later George Spink was appointed assistant manager. (See Appendix A.)

The business expanded resulting in the need for further premises as the Great Wilson Street building could not house all the machinery. Another factory was rented in Elland Road, not very far from what is now the Leeds United Football Club headquarters. There were many problems, none greater than the ones caused by the First World War.

Very early during the 1914–18 war, a disaster occurred on Good Friday, 2 April 1915 when the Elland Road works was completely gutted by fire. The whole of the paper and printed stock was destroyed, but it was found later that one or two of the machines were still usable. This was a horrifying experience for Victor Watson but immediately he put the whole of his energies into finding a way to supply his customers and keep his workpeople together. By 10am the following morning, he heard that the late Charles Russell's business, a printing company with premises in Dewsbury Road, Leeds was for sale and by 12 noon, tentative arrangements were made to purchase the business. With the help of Ralph Stephens the transaction was pushed sufficiently ahead for permission to be given to commence work in these premises straight away. During the day the Waddingtons workpeople had been rounded together and were taken to the Charles Russell building – Union Mills in Dewsbury Road – and the machines were manned and worked that same Saturday afternoon, Sunday, Easter Monday and Tuesday. The workpeople of the Charles Russell business were on holiday and their amazement when they arrived for work on the Wednesday morning must have been staggering. They found all the machines and the whole of the business manned by different people and their look of blank dismay must have had to be seen to be believed. However, aided by the war conditions with so many able-bodied people having joined the forces, John Waddington Ltd was in the position to keep both staffs fully employed. This joining of forces brought one notable addition to the company, Douglas Cameron, who was at that time a lithographic machine man and who later played a vital part in building up the success of the company. During the same year there was a first mention of the solicitors, Hepworth and Chadwick, who were employed in connection with a debt recovery and as pointed out at the start of this story, it is these little things which pave the way to future greater events.

During 1916 Victor Watson was appointed a director and from that time the company never looked back. When a search was being made for premises in London, negotiations were started with Messrs Tribe & Son, who owned a business and premises at Stoke Newington in North London. These talks were discontinued when Floral Street was found. The negotiations were started again at the end of the war and at the same time the Great Wilson Street, Leeds premises were purchased. The Tribe & Son's business was bought in January 1919 and Waddingtons were established in London in a more substantial way. George Tribe, one of the original owners, resigned due to ill health and was succeeded by Horace Watson, Victor Watson's brother. When taking over he was aided by George Spink who spent a period in London to help to put the house in order and it is understood he was christened, with typical cockney wit, 'The Silent Menace'.

Before the end of 1919 Waddingtons joined the Master Printers' Federation and early in 1920 the original Waddingtons Ltd, which was then a small business compared with the new and flourishing John Waddington Ltd, was purchased and incorporated into the company. This move strengthened the letterpress facilities and provided extra premises which were badly needed for expansion. These premises were at Camp Road and were used for the first experiments made in the manufacture of playing cards. John Waddington Ltd was thus spread out in three different areas in Leeds and two in London, but in spite of these difficulties steady progress was made in improving the quality of printing and the obtaining of orders from nationally known companies. Later in 1920 premises were rented in Bear Street, London, again in the centre of theatre land and this site was used as an office and an artist's studio. All this development required finance and at the end of 1920 it was resolved that the company should be made public and this was accomplished the following year.

The public limited company was registered on the 14 March 1921 and the first directors were:
  Edgar Lupton, described as a woollen merchant
  Arthur Copson Peake, solicitor
  Ralph Bernard Stephens, stockbroker
  Victor Hugo Watson, master printer

The first board meeting was held on 17 March 1921 when Edgar Lupton was appointed chairman and George Dixon appointed secretary. It was arranged that the registered office should be at 36 Great Wilson Street, Leeds and at this stage the following shares were issued:

35,000 £1 ordinary shares
14,250 £1 10% preference shares

About this time there was a tremendous improvement in photographic colour separation for printing and Victor Watson was one of the first to recognise that this was vital for the improvement of the quality of print which he was determined to develop. Waddingtons had accepted an order from another local printer for some chocolate box tops, because this printer was too busy to complete them in time for his customer's requirements. Victor Watson recognised the quality of the reproduction and immediately made up his mind that he must obtain the services of the person or persons concerned with this remarkable work. He found that it was Achille Vauvelle, a Frenchman who had decided to make his home in this country. Mr Vauvelle was an expert who was years ahead of his time and the fact that Victor Watson persuaded him to sign a contract with Waddingtons was a tremendous step forward in the fortunes of the company. (See Appendix B.)

In 1921 other notable happenings included the appointment of Ralph B. Stephens and Victor Watson as joint managing directors and shortly afterwards Frederick Eley, later on Sir Frederick Eley, was elected to the Board and appointed chairman. Edgar Lupton was pleased to stand down in his favour and became vice-chairman. (See Appendix C.)

In the same year of 1921 Barribal, a rather unusual artist, was contracted to work for the company and he produced many wonderful drawings which were used for posters and later for playing cards. Waddingtons had recognised the benefits of offset lithography against the direct method and were installing the modern machines becoming available in advance of many printing establishments. This combination of first-class art work reproduced photographically by Achille Vauvelle and printed under the direction of Douglas Cameron, using modern offset methods, produced a reputation for Waddingtons which was recognised.

It became apparent during 1921 that Waddingtons could not continue in the premises they were now occupying and it was resolved to purchase a large area of land in Dewsbury Road, Leeds for the purpose of building new works and offices. This plot of approximately 300,000 square feet was purchased in 1922 and plans were approved for the buildings. However, it came to the notice of the board that a factory in Hunslet, just within the Leeds boundary, which had been built by Lord Lascelles and his associates for the building of typewriters, was for sale.[2] The works and land were equivalent to the size of the Dewsbury Road plot and steps were taken to purchase, and at the same time sell the Great Wilson Street property. The purchase of the property in Hunslet was completed and on that very day, 28 September 1922, the first board meeting at Wakefield Road was held.

During 1923 Waddingtons were awarded the Blue Ribbon of the Royal Academy of British Printing for the production of prints of Mr Fred Taylor's painting of York Minster. This was a splendid tribute to the company and particularly to the wonderful reproduction work of Achille Vauvelle and the lithographic printing under the control of Douglas Cameron.

From 1905 to 1923 John Waddington Ltd had developed from a very small printing establishment with practically all their business obtained from the theatre, to a nationally known business. The quality of the printing had improved out of all recognition and was being used by large companies and important advertisers. The introduction of playing cards had made the name of the firm known beyond these shores and throughout the world and were a real turning point in the company's fortunes. Victor Watson spent much time and effort, during the years immediately following the First World War, looking for ways to increase Waddingtons' business and at the same time even out the seasonal fluctuations which made life in the printing world so difficult. He noticed that many successful large firms had specialities which called for high quality work. He believed that if he found some article based on printing, which he could sell to the general public, he could print this article when trade was slack, put it into stock and sell it all the year round. Victor Watson was a keen card player and it seemed to him that playing cards would be ideal for this purpose as they could be printed in the early part of the year when printing was usually at a low ebb.

He was strongly supported in this idea by his elder son Norman Watson who had recently joined the company. During the years 1920 and 1921 much progress was made. The circumstances were favourable, particularly so when in 1922 Charles Goodall & Co. Ltd were absorbed by Thomas De La Rue & Co. Ltd, thus leaving only one other British company in the playing card field. Playing cards had become more popular during the First World War and there

---

2 *Note by Victor Watson:* Lord Lascelles' company was known as The Conqueror Typewriter Company, a far-sighted venture which sadly did not succeed.

was a greater demand than there had been for many years. It was a fact also that playing cards were not being imported into Great Britain in any large quantity and a new and energetic approach was timely.

Waddingtons were beginning to be known as fine printers and lithographers but many things had to be accomplished before playing cards could be manufactured. It was vital to arrange that the backs of all the cards in a pack were identical so that the cards could not be identified before they were turned over. This is an essential feature of a pack of cards. It was necessary to find a reliable source for the specialised playing card material from which quality cards could be manufactured. There were the problems of getting a correct finish and cutting the cards to exactly the same size. The whole project was demanding and challenging. Norman Watson was given the task of starting the manufacture, literally on his own, and gradually built up a team of experts for what would be referred to in these days as 'a new technology'.

At the commencement the packs of playing cards were printed by direct lithography and the printing images were produced by hand transferring on to stone. The 1914–18 war had caused an acute scarcity of lithographic stones but a large supply was purchased from Germany following a personal visit by Victor Watson. These stones were of a superlative quality and were far superior to any that could be found anywhere else in the world. Victor Watson was a first class transferer but he believed that the most expert craftsman in this field was a certain Charlie Brough. He was not satisfied until he obtained this man's services and he gave Charlie Brough the job of preparing lithographic stones for playing card printing. Norman Watson vividly remembered seeing how the first stones for playing cards were prepared and these are his own words:

> The playing card images were patched up and the workmanship of Charlie Brough was so good that the register was perfect. After rolling up the image, the stone was lightly etched with nitric acid and at this stage Brough did something I had never seen before. He burned the image into the stone using a blow lamp and showed himself as a master craftsman when preparing the final process. He poured concentrated nitric acid over the whole stone and for a number of seconds it bubbled all over, not only on the non-image area, but on the printing area as well. At exactly the right moment he washed it off with water leaving a stone, which I am sure could be used for printing today if it were still in existence.

However, at this time direct lithography was rapidly changing over to offset lithography and Waddingtons, with the assistance of Achille Vauvelle and Douglas Cameron, were changing to this method well in advance of other printers. Step and repeat machines were becoming available and hand transferring was no longer required, as photographic methods were much more accurate. Early experiments were made in the Camp Road factory, but when the Wakefield Road building became available a proper manufacturing unit was set up, closely linked with the printing sections which were housed alongside.

A sales and marketing organisation was brought into existence under the leadership of Clarrie Hirst and playing cards were sold everywhere in this country and shipped in considerable quantities all over the world. The traditional way of selling playing cards through the stationery trade and to advertisers was closely examined and an entirely new concept was devised centred on selling to the stationery trade playing cards incorporating an advertisement. This became the basis of Waddingtons' 'Beautiful Britain' playing cards which depicted scenes of many seaside and country resorts. It was first subsidised by the Great Western Railway Company and later by the London and North Eastern Railway Company at a time long before the days of British Railways. It enabled beautifully printed playing cards to be sold through the stationery trade at a very low rate due to this advertising.

From then on playing cards were often in the thoughts of all concerned and it is noted that in October 1922 the Australasian Publication Company were given the sole rights for a three-year period to sell playing cards in Australia and New Zealand. This coincided with a dispute which arose with Charles Goodall & Co. with regard to the use of the word 'Linen' in connection with playing cards. This dispute seemed to be more concerned with problems in Australia than in this country, but was later amicably settled out of court. It must be agreed that 1921 and 1922 were vital years.

The amazing and rapid success in capturing a large proportion of the playing card market caused some concern to De La Rue. They believed that Waddingtons had copied the designs of their playing card faces and although these designs are traditional there is the question of copyright particularly when concerned with the ace of spades. They therefore instituted court proceedings in 1924 and sued Waddingtons on the grounds that they were 'passing off'. The case was quite protracted and it seemed that De La Rue would win and that heavy damages would be awarded against Waddingtons. However, when Waddingtons seemed on the point of losing, two exhibits were produced in court which were enlargements of the De La Rue and the Waddington aces of spades and this showed the differences to be so great that judgment was given that the Waddington ace was not a copy.

De La Rue were not happy about the decision but decided to waive an appeal and the Waddington ace was allowed to stay.

It soon became apparent that the playing card section was short of manufacturing capacity and in 1926–27 a new factory was started at Keighley, using revolutionary methods. (See Appendix D.) This factory was built for the manufacture of the standard one colour back playing cards, which were sold at low prices. At that time you could buy a perfectly good pack of playing cards for *9d.* which included the *3d.* excise duty wrapper.

THE GENERAL STRIKE

THE PERIOD FROM 1922 to the general strike in 1926 was a time for consolidation. Following the occupation of the factory in Wakefield Road, tremendous strides were made, particularly in the poster field. Waddingtons were becoming the foremost poster printers in the country and their designs were helping to advertise the products of all the leading national companies.

It was during this period that the largest poster ever printed was produced for the British Empire Exhibition, held at Wembley during 1924. This poster, which was designed by Fred Taylor, was printed as twenty-four 60 inches x 40 inches sheets and when pasted together produced a poster measuring 10 feet x 40 feet. The design showed the historical characters associated with Great Britain and was printed from twelve or thirteen colour plates. The average number of colours on each 60 inches x 40 inches sheet was ten. As there were 3,000 copies the number of impressions on this run was not far short of 1,000,000 and the order consumed ten and a half tons of paper and one and a half tons of ink. The obtaining of this order was a wonderful tribute to the technical ability for which Waddingtons were becoming famous and the actual result lived up to this reputation.

At the end of September 1924 a visit to the exhibition was organised and subsidised by the company. Practically the whole of the staff spent a day in London, having been transported from Leeds on a special train through Friday night and returning on the Saturday night. One outstanding feature of the outing was the mountain of cases of bottled beer which was loaded on to the train. Every drop was drunk before Doncaster. Victor Watson insisted on playing through the night on both journeys a new game called Buccaneer Bridge. This game was in advance of the change from Auction Bridge to Contract Bridge and could surely have been an outstanding success if Contract Bridge had not taken over.

Waddingtons were still actively engaged in the production of print for the theatrical world and it was in 1925 that the printing of the programmes for Moss Empires Ltd was placed on a contract basis subject to six months' notice on 1 June each year. This printing of Moss Empire programmes lasted for nearly forty years and was the last major connection with the theatrical world when it finished in 1963. The demands by the theatres tended to give that sense of urgency which has persisted throughout the company's history. Programmes are no use if delivered after the performance and the delivery dates were therefore sacred.

During March 1926 there was a day of jubilation at Waddingtons. The Lincolnshire Handicap of that year was run on Wednesday, 24 March, and there was a horse called the 'King of Clubs' which was trained in Yorkshire and owned by a Yorkshire farmer. It was ridden by Pat Donoghue, the fifteen-year-old son of the famous Steve Donoghue, and was never thought to have any chance at all, particularly as the Aga Khan's horse 'Zionist', the hot favourite at a price of 9–2 against, was in the race. Everybody in the factory had a small amount of money on this horse and to the amazement of all it came in by a short head in front of the twenty-six runners at a price of a 100–1. The celebrations went on far into the night and if any member of the company had followed it up by having a double on the winner of the Grand National, run two days later, he could have retired from printing altogether. This event established the fame of the playing card department inside the firm, as nothing else could possibly have done.

The general well-being of the company as well as its profitability was steadily growing until shattered by the General Strike in 1926.

The General Strike is part of our national history, but how it affected Waddingtons and how it was handled at Wakefield Road was peculiar in a number of ways.

The strike commenced at midnight on 3 May and as to be expected, with printers being strong union members all printing ceased. There were, however a number of non-union workers in the playing card department. A decision was taken to keep the works open and to allow any personnel who wanted to work to come in. To facilitate this, arrangements were made for them to sleep on the premises.

The evening before the strike started dozens of mattresses were bought from the local bedding manufacturers. Their arrival was such an unusual spectacle that a crowd of two or three thousand people gathered outside the Wakefield Road factory. It must be remembered that the works was on the fringe of the biggest coalfield in the country and the miners, who were already on strike, were more than interested to see what was happening. In the meantime people who intended to work, including the office staff, were sent home early with a promise of sleeping accommodation and meals for the duration of the strike, if they returned that evening.

On the whole it was a young community who slept on the premises, because Waddingtons' expansion had been recent and rapid which consequently meant young people joining the company in considerable numbers during the period 1922–26. In addition, because playing cards were such a new venture, practically the whole of the playing card employees were young people. In fact the average age was under thirty years. This made the plan appear to be an adventure and the whole affair a game. However, it was not a game to those who were responsible for the running of the company, because wherever possible orders had to be executed and money had to flow in to keep the firm alive. When it came to paying the people on strike for the amounts due from the previous week, Victor Watson personally interviewed and paid every man and woman and asked each individual why they had taken this action.

It was heartbreaking for him to wonder if the tremendous effort which had been made to bring the company to its present position could be jeopardised by actions which were completely beyond his control. He was particularly concerned because the rapid expansion dating from the occupation of the Wakefield Road factory had strained the finances of the company. Although he was a strong believer in unions, his faith was badly shaken and he expressed these views to some of the longer serving printers when these payments were being made.

There were many stories which could be told about the happenings in the factory during this strike period but perhaps they are best forgotten. It was recorded, however, that members of the staff struggled to produce some printing. The letterpress manager was in charge of a machine printing certain theatre posters and for some reason his assistant, Clarrie Hirst the sales manager, was underneath this same machine when it started. A serious accident was fortunately avoided but the language which issued was quite unrepeatable.

The women members of the staff did an outstanding service for the workers who stayed and slept on the premises. A remarkable letter written by Mrs Norman Watson (who at the time was a secretary at Wakefield Road) has been preserved. (See Appendix E.)

This letter helps to give an authentic picture of what was happening at Wakefield Road during that momentous time. To the working community it was more like a holiday camp. A good eight hours work was given by all but then followed an evening of entertainment. There was a piano and a gramophone enabling a dance to be organised each evening. There was table tennis and naturally playing cards available. To many, the end of the strike was not wanted as they enjoyed themselves so well. However, the strike was over on Wednesday, 12 May after nine days, and this remarkable state of affairs both at Waddingtons and throughout the country was a thing of the past which was best forgotten as quickly as possible.

Once the General Strike was over a stupendous effort was made to put the effects on one side and to return to normal. This was difficult because apart from the many outside repercussions there was a loss of confidence between the management and the employees which took years to repair. Throughout industry there was a harder approach to the question of shortage of work and instead of keeping people employed on other jobs when orders were not available, short-time working and notices to finish were the order of the day.

However, in spite of the continuation of the coal strike and the occasional shortage of electrical power, Waddingtons remained busy and there were very few dismissals. All the time, better and better quality printing work was being produced and this advancement was effected without neglecting to maintain the theatrical programmes and posters. The theatre business was increased, in fact at the beginning of 1927 a contract was negotiated for the printing of programmes for the famous London Savoy Theatre, the original home of the d'Oyly Carte Operas, for a period of seven years. This great effort to improve and to expand demanded more finance and in 1928 the capital of the company was substantially increased by issuing more ordinary shares and also 7.5% preference shares.

During this same year the company purchased a two-colour double demy offset lithographic machine from George Mann & Co. Ltd which introduced steel cylinders for the first time. The making of machines with steel cylinders and later steel beds, proved to be an error of judgment and caused a serious problem for Manns and made a lot of trouble at Waddingtons. However, certain lithographic machine minders, headed by Len Watkinson, were adamant that this machine was not right and their insistence saved the company from much of the trouble which was experienced by very many lithographic printers, not only in this country but all over the world. During this period Ted Dodsworth, who worked for Manns, was extremely helpful and spent many hours with the Waddington personnel trying to make this machine work satisfactorily. When the opportunity arose, which was many years later, he joined the company and was responsible for many of the engineering improvements on the playing card and packaging sides of the business.

Rapid progress was being made at the Keighley playing card factory, now with a resident manager, Fred Harrison, and very soon the production reached 10,000 packs per week, rising quickly to 30,000 packs per week and making inroads into the market held by Thomas De La Rue. Early in 1929 the production of a circular pack of cards was started at the Leeds Factory and these were accepted by the general public and sold in huge quantities. They were introduced to the United States of America where sales were far beyond expectation. To cope with the tremendous demand a double-day shift was introduced for the girls working the playing card machinery. Shift work up to this time had always been a day shift and a night shift but as this was out of the question for girls, the hours were arranged from 6am to 2pm and 2pm to 10pm, in a similar way to the present day printing double-day shifts.

Later in 1929 a merger took place which improved out of all recognition the quality and service of the letterpress section of the business. A well run and attractive letterpress works owned by J. A. Stembridge, trading under the name of Stembridge & Co. Ltd, was taken over by Waddingtons and the machinery brought to Wakefield Road. Over the years Waddingtons had tended to improve the lithographic plant at the expense of the letterpress machinery and this merger righted the balance to the benefit of the business as a whole. The machinery from Mr Stembridge's factory was extremely modern and included a number of American printing machines and the most up-to-date type-setting equipment available. New life was brought into the business, although as often happens with mergers there were clashes of personalities which took a long time to resolve.

James Stembridge was a great believer in the Master Printers' costing methods and introduced them to Waddingtons at a time when this kind of change was badly needed. The alteration in method was not done without opposition but it was greatly helped by the methodical approach to the whole question by George Spink. It was decided to form an Auxiliary Board of Directors, a kind of junior board who could look after the day-to-day running of the business, particularly from a production angle. The first members of this board were Messrs George Spink, J. A. Stembridge, Douglas A. Cameron and Norman V. Watson and they met once every two weeks, later amended to once every four weeks.

It was the Auxiliary Board who recommended in 1931 the purchase of the first carton cutting and creasing machine. The strange fact is that when it was delivered this machine was not used for its original purpose for over twelve months. The first year of its life it ran day and night cutting miniature playing cards for inserting into cigarette packets. This vital part of the 'Wills' Scheme' was a valuable contribution to the remarkable period of prosperity enjoyed by Waddingtons during the worst period of the slump.

Before this purchase took place, the country as a whole was running into trading difficulties and although Waddingtons remained busy it was a time of savage price cutting and reductions in profits. It was the start of the slump years and many improvements had to be shelved. Victor Watson and his directors struggled to find new avenues for business and a severe economy campaign was instituted. This with other measures helped to keep the company solvent.

This economy campaign did not prevent an extension being made at the Stoke Newington factory by the addition of three large bays. This extra building was started in January 1931, with the knowledge that the small factory in the heart of theatre land in Floral Street was shortly due to be closed. In fact the plant and machinery were transferred to Stoke Newington in September of the same year.

For some years Victor Watson had advocated the formation of a pension scheme to safeguard the interest of the staff, the managers and the foremen. He hoped that this would be extended to all employees at some time when finance made it possible. He was a great admirer of Lloyd George and his own liberal outlook caused him great personal sorrow when the pension proposal had to be put on one side due to the difficult days which the company was experiencing. It took fourteen years and the stresses of the Second World War before the scheme could be revived and it was another indication of the business difficulties experienced in the early thirties.

The tremendous increase in the cinema and the making of silent films had hardly affected the live theatre but the introduction of the talkie, first shown in Great Britain in 1930, was greatly feared. This helped to direct Waddingtons' policy towards the curtailing of theatrical printing and expanding in other directions. Much progress was made in the producing of pictorial posters and Waddingtons became the foremost poster printing company in the country, supplying national advertisers such as Reckitts, Unilever, and the various breweries. The excellence of these posters was recognised throughout the advertising world and brought more and more work of this description.

Douglas Cameron was taken seriously ill in 1930, but he fully recovered and was able to continue with the controlling of the expansion of the firm's lithographic work which new methods and new machinery were making possible. Everything seemed set for a great future but was held back by the excessive competition caused by the general rundown of industry and commerce as a whole. It was indeed a period of poor trading conditions, but Waddingtons were facing the same problems as the country throughout.

Point-of-sale advertising had increased considerably and the company made great strides to take advantage of this situation. Efforts were made to sell showcards of all descriptions and this linked up very well with the poster work. The customers were the same and very often it could mean using a reduction of the design used on a poster. At the same time early experiments were made in the production of cartons using the letterpress machinery which came with the addition of Stembridge & Co. and the knowledge of some of their craftsmen. Discussions were started with our agents in Australia for the manufacture of playing cards in Sydney and although the deal came to nothing it showed how lively the company was in trying to find new business. Instead of employing an agent to sell playing cards in India it was decided to engage Selby Wilson to carry out this work direct.

These ideas and many more were tried in an effort to combat the serious contraction of trade Waddingtons were suffering.

In spite of these tremendous efforts, the first half of Waddingtons' financial year ending 30 September 1931 showed a trading loss and in common with many other companies Waddingtons had to make severe economies, even to the point of making a reduction in staff salaries. Gloom in the industrial world grew to alarming proportions but Waddingtons were on the point of entering one of the most prosperous periods of their existence.

The second half of 1931 was economically disastrous for the country as a whole and seemed likely to be equally disastrous for Waddingtons. The second Socialist Government was running into trouble following a world wide slump which had a particularly severe effect in the United States of America. At the end of July 1931 Philip Snowden, the Chancellor of the Exchequer, admitted that the financial position of Great Britain was serious. World commodity prices slumped alarmingly, particularly cotton on which the Lancashire economy was still so dependent, and unemployment in Lancashire rose rapidly.

The Government proposed drastic economy measures which included a cut in unemployment pay. The TUC revolted against such a suggestion and this culminated in the fall of the Socialist Government and the formation of a National Administration on 25 August 1931. Taxes on beer, tobacco and petrol were increased; income tax, too, went up. This seems laughable today when the higher income tax demanded was 5/- in the £, against the previous rate of 4/6. Finally on 20 September 1931 Great Britain was forced off the gold standard which had the effect of devaluing our currency and putting up the cost of living, and finally in 1932 the age-long policy of free trade was abandoned and import tariffs were introduced.

During these critical months Waddingtons, as was the case in the whole of industry, faced grave difficulties. Competition for print orders reached a desperate state. Prices were cut, profits fell and the work-force had to be reduced. Just before Christmas 1931, Victor Watson called together the whole of his staff and asked them to accept a reduction of 10% and led the way by accepting a 20% reduction himself. This drastic action helped to bridge the gap to keep the company solvent, but a wonderful change of fortune for Waddingtons took place early in 1932.

There have been many milestones in the history of this company but the one which made the greatest impact and built a solid foundation for the future was the Wills' playing card scheme. The idea was to insert miniature playing cards into all packs of cigarettes instead of the customary cigarette cards. The recipients were invited to collect a full pack of fifty-three cards which they could exchange for a super quality, normal sized pack of cards. The enquiry for the cards was received from Wills when Victor Watson was in London. As the same enquiry had been sent to the other makers of playing cards he knew that there was no time to lose and therefore made an appointment to see the people at Wills in Bristol two days later. In Leeds, Norman Watson had to prepare the samples which, by the time they were finished, were truly wonderful.

The fateful meeting was arranged for 10am. Victor Watson travelled overnight from London and Norman Watson from Leeds and they met at a Bristol hotel for breakfast to discuss tactics. The samples were in a number of suitcases travelling with Norman Watson. At 9pm the previous evening they were still unfinished but were at such an advanced stage that Norman Watson thought he would go home for a meal and prepare to catch the midnight train for Bristol. The bulk of the samples were already in his possession, but certain final samples – and very important ones – were left to be brought down from the Wakefield Road factory to the midnight train. Unfortunately the bearer of these samples left it so late that all transport had finished and the obtaining of a taxi was impossible. Taxis in Leeds in the thirties were few and far between as indeed were private cars – even to try and hitch a lift was a problem but in those days tramcars were still running and by a stroke of good fortune there was a tramcar at the Thwaite Gate terminus, 200 yards from the factory.

The conductor was a pianist in the local dance band who had appeared at a Waddingtons function two or three days earlier. The normal travelling time by tramcar from the Thwaite Gate terminus to the centre of Leeds was, according to the timetable, twelve minutes and the train was due to leave in ten minutes. The conductor persuaded the driver that they could do the trip in six minutes, and they set off with their one and only passenger and his bag of samples. A sprint from the tram to the station and a side-step round the ticket-collector enabled the remaining samples to be handed through the window of the moving train to Norman Watson. It was perhaps fortunate that the central figure in this drama was a young and active rugby player![3] Many of the fancy boxes for the cards were made by Stones of Banbury and a number of new ones had been prepared for the presentation to Wills. A representative of Stones met the Bristol train at Birmingham and Norman Watson then set about boxing and packing the cards so that by the time the train reached Bristol he was ready for breakfast and briefing. Such was the start of the greatest contract ever handled by Waddingtons.

Wills were so impressed and delighted that they placed substantial orders, far greater than the two Watsons ever expected. The scheme was restricted to four cigarette lines – Woodbines, Capstan, Star and Gold Flake. When the scheme really developed the sales of these cigarettes increased tremendously whereas the sales of all other brands fell off. Waddingtons bought their first cutting and creasing machine for the making of folding cards, yet this machine never made a carton for twelve months because it was working night and day cutting the miniature cards which went into the cigarette packets. These cards were manufactured at the rate of 5,000,000 per week and some were eventually printed and finished by Wills themselves.

The exciting time came when the general public started to send for the standard packs of playing cards which were well designed, beautifully printed and elegantly boxed. The demand grew at an alarming rate, far beyond the normal output of the playing card factory. The stationery trade were horrified because they said that Waddingtons were ruining their business. There was a lot of heart-searching amongst the Waddingtons playing card representatives and playing card selling staff who thought that the end of the world had come.

Victor Watson tried to allay their fears because he said he was sure that this scheme would have the long-term effect of making people conscious that they wanted to play with a new and clean pack of cards. This proved to

---

3   Doug Brearley, the writer of this account.

be a correct forecast, because when on average every household in Great Britain eventually obtained one or more of these packs they became used to playing with new cards. In the meantime, the factory had never been busier, even though slump conditions were still prevailing.

Wills and Waddingtons had never realised that the collection and exchanging of small cards could reach such tremendous proportions. For example, it became general in public houses to see a receptacle placed on the bar counter full of Wills miniature cards. People came in and exchanged their own cards for ones they needed to make up a pack. This system accelerated the completion of packs although it seemed certain that sets were sent in which were not of the correct sequence although the required number. How Wills dealt with this problem is not recorded but it is thought they must have ignored it and sent out the super packs without further query.

One of Wills' stipulations was that all the playing cards should have gold edges, and very soon this became a bottle-neck because gold edging was a hand operation carried out by skilled craftsmen who, even in those days were a dying race. Soon every known craftsman in the country was working on the gold edging of playing cards. A breaking point had to come. Although we experimented with a more automatic method of putting on a gold edge and opened a small factory in Rothwell nearby for this purpose, we could not cope. The opening of this factory had one important benefit. It found a number of people who, once they were members of Waddingtons, stayed and joined us in our later activities. Of these, two outstanding individuals were the Taylor brothers – Hugh and Ronnie.

Eventually Wills had to compromise by supplying bridge sets to people who collected six and twelve of these miniature packs. They even supplied bridge tables and other equipment which naturally Waddingtons were not keen about because it was away from their own manufacture. The other cigarette manufacturers tried to compete by the introduction of coupons but in due time an agreement was made that all types of coupon/card trading should finish. However this had to be phased out gradually and before it was ended Waddingtons had made such profits that they were able to develop in other directions from the sound base this activity had created.

THE BEGINNING OF EXPANSION

THERE WERE THREE main developments, all put under the capable direction of Norman Watson. First the making of folding cartons, second the cutting and packing of cardboard jigsaw puzzles, and third the start of games manufacture.

There was a growing demand for folding cartons, particularly by the Unilever Companies headed by Lever Brothers of Port Sunlight, who required millions of display outers and wanted to produce a series for Lux soap and Lifebuoy soap showing heads of cinema stars. The need was for high quality printing to suit these beautiful girls' heads but on folding boxboard of a type which could be made into cartons. Waddingtons were producing quality show cards using the excellent reproduction work of the Vauvelle family and high-class printing under the leadership of Douglas Cameron. This was being recognised by all the leading national advertisers which led Lever Brothers to believe that Waddingtons could meet their requirements.

The first efforts in carton making yielded poor results. The printing rubbed too easily to withstand the later processes. The cartons were not cut accurately enough and the problem of handling heavy board was quite different from handling paper. First experiments in cutting were made on letterpress machines using letterpress techniques of forme-making, but later more modern methods were introduced and after many struggles cartons were produced acceptable to the very critical Lever Brothers buyers.

It became evident that the carton cutting formes were neither economically made nor accurate enough for the required purpose. In fact, the whole operation needed information of a kind which would improve the techniques which were entirely different from those of printing.

Jim Allen was appointed as a foreman and he was able to introduce Waddingtons to many of the methods being used by other companies. He was an excellent craftsman. He could make sample cartons by hand with wonderful accuracy and speed and was able to make cutters using plywood and cutting steel bought from Sweden. Jim Allen's efforts were supported by Len Grimston and Sam Render and the making of cartons was put on a sound basis. Allen, whose character did not match his technical ability, disappeared from the scene following an internal dispute, but very soon Waddingtons were receiving orders from national companies, particularly in the confectionery trade. The entry into the carton field was into the quality side of the industry mainly relating to foodstuffs.

Rapid development took place and further machinery was obtained including fast-running glueing machines bought from America. A young energetic sales representative, Harry Bradley, was engaged and he brought with him knowledge and experience of selling cartons. He was able to negotiate a large contract with Messrs F. & A. Parkinson of Guiseley for electric lamp cartons, and this with other orders enabled the firm to buy folding boxboard on a much better basis both from this country and abroad. It was at this point of time that Waddingtons became big buyers of carton board from Finland and have remained so ever since, apart from the short gap during the Second World War.

The carton section grew very rapidly and within a short period became the largest department in the company with the highest turnover. Its development was helped by the introduction of the Satona waxed milk container which demanded a high standard of accuracy. This was to a degree in advance of the precisions demanded by the commercial customers but when their requirements needed this accuracy Waddingtons were in a position to comply. The Satona waxed carton business, however, was started in 1936 and is a story in itself, but the making of cardboard jigsaws came before this development.

An American company (probably Einson Freeman) in Long Island, New York, developed a method of making jigsaw puzzles using cardboard instead of wood. As might be expected from the name, jigsaws were originally cut out by a jigsaw. This new idea no longer required a saw. It enabled the puzzles to be made at a twentieth of the cost and started a craze in the United States, which later arrived in this country.

Waddingtons bought the 'know how' and one or two machines from America in the summer of 1933 and commenced to manufacture and sell through a distributor, Louis Marx, a company operating in the toy trade. Louis Marx sold the whole of the output to Woolworths and the craze grew to such proportions that it became difficult to cope with the demand. Although the 'know how' was obtained from America, the early problems were quite staggering. The reproduction and the printing of the pictures was easy, the making of the cartons for holding the jigsaws was also easy, both being part of the normal Waddingtons practice. It was when the time came to cut them out and break them up that the trouble started. The giant cutting press required a tremendous amount of pressure, due to the fact that the pieces of a jigsaw must be held together when cut and could not be broken up until later. The early trials resulted in cracking the machine head and breaking some of the steel posts which were the thickness of a man's arm and which took the strain of the cutting operation. However, this problem was solved when Victor Watson Senior decided to try the skill and ingenuity of a letterpress printer to 'make ready' the cutting in the same way as making ready a letterpress half-tone print. The man concerned was Sid Benson. He joined the company when J. A. Stembridge & Co. Ltd merged with Waddingtons, and from the moment he took over the preparation work before cutting, good results were obtained.

Later, however, disagreements took place between the marketing people, Louis Marx and Waddingtons. Their managing director was scared that the craze for jigsaws would finish and would not place forward orders of a sufficient size to enable the manufacture to have a continuous flow. This made the management of the manufacturing side nigh impossible and later Mr Watson decided that Waddingtons should market jigsaws through the stationery trade, because he was convinced that it was not a dying craze and that cardboard puzzles would always sell at a price lower than those made of wood. This prediction proved to be correct and jigsaw puzzles are sold today in even higher quantities than during the 'craze' period.

During the time of the introduction of cartons and of jigsaw puzzles another change was taking place which was developing much more slowly. A writer by the name of David Whitelaw persuaded the company to produce and sell a word game – Lexicon. This was basically a pack of cards but with the faces changed from court cards and pips to letters of the alphabet. The summer of 1933 saw the introduction of this game, when a small edition was produced and sold to test the market. This was the first Waddingtons game and its introduction had an unsuccessful beginning. The first edition was sold through the stationery shops at 1*s*. 9*d*. each and sales were practically non-existent. It was decided to pack Lexicon more attractively and raise the price to 2*s*. 6*d*. per pack. This was an unprecedented approach in the stationery world and there was much opposition and criticism. However, when the real launching took place in the autumn, heralded by an intensive newspaper advertising campaign, sales, instead of being a hundred a month were thousands a day, and there was a wonderful success which has continued up to the present time.[4]

On a certain Friday night towards the end of 1935, Victor Watson Senior handed Norman Watson a game with the remark 'Look this over and tell me what you think about it.' It is recorded that Norman Watson said:

> I played an imaginary game against myself continuing through Friday night, Saturday night and Sunday night. I was enthralled and captivated. I had

---

4 1973

never found a game so absorbing, and thus Monopoly was first played in England at my home. I was so enthusiastic that on the Monday morning I persuaded my father to make a telephone call to Parker Brothers of Salem, Mass., USA, the holder of the rights. Today transatlantic telephone calls are commonplace, but this was the first one ever made by Waddingtons and I was told it was the first one ever received by Parker Brothers from Europe, so that, apart from its far-reaching consequences, the call itself was something of a landmark.

Monopoly was invented in Pennsylvania by an unemployed heating engineer called Charles B. Darrow, who died in 1967. He developed it from a 1924 game called 'Landlord' created by a Virginian lady, Elizabeth Phillips, as propaganda for tax reform. Mr Darrow had great difficulties in persuading any manufacturer to use his idea but when Parker Brothers eventually took it over it was an immediate and wonderful success. Waddingtons were granted a licence to manufacture and ever since the company has been know to the general public as 'the Monopoly people'.

When thinking and deciding how to change this American game into a British game by altering the names of the New York streets to London streets a number of Waddingtons executives became so engrossed that they were playing the game instead of working. Wherever Monopoly was played the players found they could not leave it alone and it became an addiction. The names of the streets and railway stations were the only alterations made. The rules were left, like the rules of chess, unchanged; and although values of properties are so different today, when Waddingtons have been asked to alter Monopoly values the answer has always been 'no'.

In January 1935 a financial interest was obtained in Dublin when Waddingtons made a part acquisition of the Ormond Printing Company. This enabled the firm to extend their activities in Ireland, particularly by manufacturing playing cards and making cartons in Dublin.

Whilst all this was proceeding the print was all the time being improved and new markets found. The company were asked to print labels for Heinz, who had very recently started to manufacture in this country. Their demands for high quality labels helped to improve the standards and the very fact that Waddingtons were able to say that they were printers for Heinz was an advertisement in itself. These were the days of expansion leading up to the Second World War. A further major development, the manufacture of the Satona Container, came about as follows.

Very soon after the First World War the distribution of milk was completely altered by the use of the glass bottle. During the period between the two wars attempts were made to introduce a paper container, with varying success. In the early thirties an idea from Denmark for using paper and paraffin wax was introduced into this country when a company, Satona Ltd, was formed in Scotland in 1933. The directors were Richard G. Thyne, William Thyne Junior, Carl W. Hartman and Louis M. Hartman. The two Hartmans were the Danish inventors of the Satona system and the Thynes were connected with Thynes of Edinburgh, carton manufacturers.

The idea behind this development was for Satona Ltd to supply machinery to dairies for the making up, waxing, filling and closing of Satona containers, and to licence various carton manufacturers to supply the blanks. To make it suitable for smaller dairies a tapered carton was developed, which could be waxed by the carton manufacturer and supplied nested to the dairy.

It was resolved that the company should concentrate on equipment adapted primarily for milk, oil and semi-liquids such as syrup, and to concentrate on the following countries: Great Britain, Denmark, Holland, Sweden, France, Canada and the USA. The early days of this company were far from easy and there was difficulty in finding a suitable licensee for the rest of Great Britain, although William Thyne of Edinburgh held the licence for Scotland.

Waddingtons first became interested in the Satona system in 1936 when they were invited to become licensees for the rest of Great Britain. At the same time they were asked to invest money in Satona Ltd which was in some financial difficulty, but the Waddingtons directors were against this part of the venture.

Victor Watson Senior, however, was so certain that the idea could be a success that he invested his own personal money and at the same time persuaded Rupert Hicks, whom he had recently met, to buy shares in this project. Victor Watson became chairman of Satona Ltd, his son Norman Watson, became a director, and Rupert Hicks was made secretary.

Waddingtons' carton making had improved but the demand for a leak-proof container to be made up in dairies (which needed a foolproof system) made it essential that the cartons were perfect. In this way Waddingtons' carton department was forced into making more accurate cartons than most of their competitors and thus became ahead in this field. This was an extra bonus to the profits made from selling Satona cartons.

1937 saw a short-lived steep increase in the price of paper which tended to make for difficulties, particularly in this new waxed container business.

In spite of this an extension to the Wakefield Road factory was planned and built mainly to house the additional machinery needed for the Satona project and in October 1937, contracts were placed with J. H. Wood & Co. Ltd for the building, Bannister and Walton for the steelwork, and Concrete Ltd for the floors.

The first machinery was made in Denmark in the Hartmans' own factory, but it was soon found that this engineering works was unable to cope with the demand and it was arranged for additional machinery to be made in Bristol by Beasley French & Co., who for a long time had been associated with Waddingtons. Later the Forgrove Machinery Company of Leeds were persuaded to make a number of machines and during this period Axel Holmburg, a clever Danish engineer, came to Leeds to help with this expansion, installing machinery made at the Hartman factory in Denmark. The first big dairy installation in this country was at Mortlocks in London but there were other installations in Toronto, Canada and Johannesburg, South Africa. The Oldham Co-Operative Society placed an order for a machine for making 1/3 pint milk containers for supplying to schools and the whole development was progressing very well. The Independent Dairies and Blaydon Dairies of London were about to buy machinery but were stopped by the commencement of the Second World War. Before the war Rupert Hicks had arranged through the Crown Agents of the Colonies to sell a machine to Malta and everything seemed set for success until the war escalated in 1940, bringing grave difficulties in the supply of paper and paraffin wax.

The factory extensions were finished in 1938 when a substantial department for the waxing of the tapered style of carton was started, the manager being Jim Brough, an international rugby union player who also became an international rugby league player. He gave up his rugby career to help Norman Watson to put the making of Satona cartons on a firm basis. It was during this year that Waddingtons received a severe blow from the death of James Stembridge, who died suddenly on 28 October 1938.

Mr Stembridge was the head of the company, J. A. Stembridge & Co. Ltd, which merged with Waddingtons in 1929, and he later joined the Board. He was a strong supporter of Victor Watson in his efforts to develop the Satona system and the loss of Mr Stembridge at this stage was a setback to the company's progress in the milk distribution field.

During the early part of 1939 tremendous stocks of paper and paraffin wax were bought in anticipation of a shortage, which became acute when Norway was invaded and the manufacture and use of paper was very strictly controlled by the Government. However, assistance was given where paper was used for the supply of milk containers but in spite of this the rising costs made for additional problems. Efforts were made to alleviate costs by persuading advertisers to buy the space of one of the panels of the milk containers and this was used by companies whose advertising was restricted in other directions. As packing materials became more restricted the Satona containers were used for other foods and considerable help was given to Messrs Bengers Ltd for making and supplying a container to hold junket powder. The paper used in this instance was made from straw which caused many problems due to the poor quality and the dirty colour of the finished article. Improvements were gradually made and eventually an attractive and reasonable container was supplied and used in considerable quantities.

Satona went on to be a great business justifying Victor Watson's early faith in it but as he died in 1943 he never saw his vision fulfilled.

The First World War brought problems, trials and difficulties to a young firm struggling hard to find its feet. However, the outbreak of the Second World War found a greatly expanded business with a production capacity enormously increased and growing rapidly. It became evident in the early part of 1939 that war was inevitable and a number of preparations were made, some with the idea of making sure of survival of the business and some which were as a result of direct instructions from the Government. The stocks of paper and board were increased enormously. The basement of the Leeds building was converted into a giant air raid shelter and an Air Raid Precautions section was formed in the company. This included the training and equipping of a works fire brigade guided by a retired fire brigade officer and men were trained in methods of decontamination to combat the results of the use of poison gas. Poison gas was not used during the war but there was a tremendous fear throughout the whole population about the use of gas and precautions were taken. Later a fire watching squad was formed but this was only in line with what all factories and commercial houses had to do, particularly in the areas where bombing became heavy.

The fact that the war was about to start was brought home to many people when they found that their menfolk were being called up to the Armed Forces. Members of the Territorial Army were high on the list and a week before war was declared two of Waddingtons personnel were called to duty. Clem Dobson was the first, followed a few hours later by Charles Moore. The following day Bert Allen and others were called and before the actual declaration was made, seventeen of Waddingtons' staff were already in uniform. The writer vividly remembers the impact of this news because he was in Victor Watson Senior's office when Douglas Cameron came in to tell Mr Watson that the first man had left. As this was the writer's brother-in-law and as it was the first knowledge he had of such a happening it can be understood why the news was so startling.

It was soon recognised that the printed word had become a war weapon, not only in the accepted field of propaganda, but in very many unusual and dramatic ways. The first thing that happened was that Waddingtons were asked to produce some low denomination banknotes, valued at *2s. 6d.* and *5s.* (today's equivalent 12½p and 25p) to take the place of coins. These notes were produced under very strict security arrangements and only the people actually working on them knew that they were being printed.

This was Waddingtons' first contact with the Bank of England which has lasted for the mutual benefit of both ever since. These notes were never issued and were kept on Waddingtons premises for a number of years before being taken over by the Government for destruction.

Due to the lines along which the business had been developing it had built up substantial resources of 'know-how' in the highly specialised processes of printing and packaging and those in charge of our country's war efforts were not slow to recognise the value of such skill and experience. Very early in the war Waddingtons found themselves involved in activities of an extremely diverse and highly confidential nature. This was in the field of the specialised printing of secret documents of all kinds, including maps of every part of the world. Some of these maps were printed on large silk squares for which special treatments were necessary to ensure that the material would not stretch nor the design be otherwise affected by extraordinary physical or climatic conditions.

In addition fascinating projects were carried out, many by word of mouth instructions only from the authorities to Norman Watson. This was in connection with printing and printed supplies used by the Secret Service, but the full extent will never be known and in any case could not be published.

During the first few months of the war Waddingtons' normal printing business was drastically curtailed due to lack of demand but the company were fortunate in having good stocks of playing cards and games which sold so well that the company's financial position was maintained. At the same time the Satona container side of the business was extremely busy. However, what could have been a major disaster happened on the 15 April 1940 when the contents of the paraffin wax store caught fire and considerable quantities of paper stocks were badly damaged. Fortunately the fire was contained to one outbuilding, although for some time it could easily have extended to the main factory.

The newly formed Air Raid Precautions fire brigade did a valiant job of preventive work until the city fire brigade arrived.

Two stories are worth telling about the happenings during the fire. An eye witness can be quoted as follows:

'The City Chief Fire Officer, using his authority to keep sightseers away, very abruptly demanded that Victor Watson should come right away. The reply was typical:

"Whose bloody fire do you think this is?"'

Very shortly after this incident Mr Watson ordered the buyer, who was also watching the conflagration, to go away and make strenuous efforts to obtain further supplies of paraffin wax, even while the fire was still burning.

Before the commencement of hostilities, arrangements had been made between the De La Rue Company and John Waddington Ltd, that if either suffered damage by enemy action at any one of their factories the other company would help with the production difficulties which would accrue.

In December 1940 the De La Rue main factory was completely gutted during the first big London fire raid and within days Waddingtons were printing and finishing foreign banknotes which had been the main output of this particular factory. Although playing cards, also produced in these buildings, had never been mentioned, or even thought about, when the two managing directors met together at the burned out site with the remains still smouldering, a characteristic gesture was made by Victor Watson, who said:

'For every pack of cards produced for John Waddington we shall manufacture one for De La Rue.'

This happening brought about a reorganisation of Waddingtons' activities and led to them rendering very valuable assistance to De La Rue in their banknote printing business. A large proportion of Waddingtons' litho printing machines were continually engaged on the initial printing of banknotes sheets prior to their transfer to the De La Rue department for further processing and finishing operations. Large areas of factory space were made available to the De La Rue Company for the installation of specialised machinery for direct plate printing and to accommodate the many hundreds of employees who were engaged in the production of foreign currency. Despite continuous air and sea attacks on our ships, many hundreds of millions of banknotes from Leeds continued throughout the war to be sent to countries all over the world. In addition large quantities of banknotes were printed for various European countries which were intended to be put into circulation as a temporary issue following the departure of the German occupation forces.

All banknote production in Leeds and subsequently in the Gateshead factories came under the control of the De La Rue resident manager, Mr Claxton Prudhoe.

A company was formed for the manufacture of playing cards for De La Rue and Waddingtons, leaving the selling and distribution to them both. All these activities had to be put on a semi-permanent basis and lasted for years after the war had finished.

Before long various government departments, looking for additional factories for war service production, visited Wakefield Road and were seemingly anxious to cut down all printing activities. However, by this time, in addition to the banknote printing, which was looked at very favourably by the Treasury, Waddingtons had started to print maps, which were mentioned earlier in the chapter, and had made an agreement with ICI Metals Ltd to lease part of the factory for the production of cartridge cases used for Verey lights and mortar bombs.

The silk maps, which were beautifully printed, of areas of Germany, Austria, Italy and France, were mainly used as escape maps and were put inside the linings of Air Force uniforms.[5] This fact was never known by anyone in Waddingtons until years later. The whole of the work was done under the strictest security and a singular thing about the instructions for the maps was that very rarely was anything put in writing.

The ICI Metals Department, although under ICI control, was worked by Waddingtons personnel who were loaned to ICI for the period of the operation.

A tremendous change was taking place which meant the reduction in size of the games department and of the carton department, which finally had its production towards the end of 1942 concentrated at Field Son & Co. Ltd, Bradford.

The company was allowed to keep the making of the blanks for the Satona operation and continued with this work throughout the period of the war. This keeping of some carton cutting machinery enabled one million 24-hour ration boxes to be made towards the end of 1943, and was no doubt a further contribution by the company to D-Day which took place in June the following year.

These boxes were cut and creased on the normal machinery and made up on a chocolate box machine borrowed from Messrs Cadbury. They were then paraffin waxed in a contraption built specially for the job, as the Satona machinery could not handle a square box and lid of this type.

---

5 *Note by Victor Watson:* Very little silk was used for the printing of escape maps. Most of them were on rayon. However, they were always called silk maps.

From the moment Norway was invaded the paper shortage, which was already serious, became acute. All paper supplies were strictly licensed for particular purposes and economies were demanded in every possible way. Cartons had the material reduced in calliper and labels for cans were directed to be reduced to a very narrow strip, and as far as games were concerned no paper at all was granted for this purpose.

This prohibition extended to playing cards. In the early days of the war playing cards were regarded as superfluous and the material to make them became more and more difficult to obtain. Finally, however, it was the personal intervention of Mr Winston Churchill which brought the position to a head when he was visiting the troops in Egypt.

In Volume V of Churchill's *Memoirs of the Second World War* there is printed a memo from the Prime Minister to the President of the Board of Trade, which reads as follows:

> Prime Minister to the Board of Trade.
> 26 July 1943
> I am told that in spite of contributions from civilian supplies there is at present a shortage of playing cards for use by the forces and workers in industry. The importance of providing amusement for the forces in their leisure hours and in long periods of waiting and monotony in out of the way places, and for the sailors penned up in their ships for months together, cannot be overstated. Nothing is more handy, more portable, or more capable of prolonged usage than a pack of cards.
> Let me have a report on this subject, and show me how you can remedy this deficiency. It ought to mean only a microscopic drain on our resources to make a few hundred thousand packs.

A further extract from the Prime Minister to the President of the Board of Trade reads as follows:

> Prime Minister to the Board of Trade.
> 1 August 1943
> The important thing is to have cards freely forthcoming when called for, and although the soldiers should have priority civilian workers need them too.

The following comment was made by Norman Watson in November 1952, when he recalled this situation:

The outcome in 1943, was that the President of the Board of Trade sent for me to discuss the whole position. But by this time the horse had bolted; in other words our stock of playing card board was exhausted and our experienced staff had been absorbed into other industries. However, as many of us know the position did improve slightly. A few girls were allowed to return to the playing card industry, and certain materials were allocated to us. All who lived through these stirring times will remember that when Mr Churchill gave an order it had to be carried out and although we were completely unequipped for any return to normal manufacturing programmes, something had to be done, and was done.

During this time all the men under thirty-five years of age were called up for active service and a number of the girls were also either directed to the Women's Auxiliary Services or munition factories. However, the girls working on the banknote side and in the department started by ICI Metals Ltd were allowed to stay, which meant there was a nucleus of trained people available for when the wartime activities ceased.

Leeds was fortunate in suffering very little bomb damage and the only raid of any consequence was in the spring of 1941. The nearest bomb to fall in the vicinity of our Wakefield Road factory was at least half a mile away and the production was never interrupted.

The reason for the creation of an ICI Metals section in Leeds was the need for having production dispersed in different parts of the country. This was the country's general policy so that production could still proceed even if one particular factory suffered severe bomb damage. For this reason Waddingtons opened a factory on the Team Valley Estate at Gateshead-on-Tyne for the finishing, in connection with De La Rue, of the growing quantities of foreign banknotes. The first small factory was obtained alongside, but it was some years before the move to the present Gateshead factory, which is now fully occupied and producing quality labels of all descriptions.

Before this development took place Douglas Cameron was elected a director in February 1941 and in November of the following year Cyril Stephens was also elected a director. In December 1943, however, the death of Victor Watson, whose lifelong energy and progressive policy had been so largely responsible for the company's prosperity, was a grievous blow. His personality had infused such earnestness and vitality into all the workpeople and staff that the growth of the company had seemed inevitable. To all who worked for him and with him he was a wonderful friend and leader.

CHAPTER THREE

VICTOR WATSON'S OWN ACCOUNT

(TAKEN FROM THE *WADDINGTON TEAM*
MAGAZINES OF 1927 AND 1928)

March 1927
Dear readers,

WHEN THE SUGGESTION was made by Mr Joe Forrest that a *Bulletin* or *House Organ* or *Works' Magazine* should be published, I was very surprised and inclined to smile, but as I turned the matter over in my mind, I became convinced that this suggestion was one of the best suggestions that had been brought forward, therefore I grasped the opportunity, because I could plainly see that it provided a means whereby the management could keep in closer touch with all the people who were following them, and also the followers could keep in touch with the management, and I contend that the closer the relationship becomes between the managers of the various branches and the rank and file, it will be better for the firm, and the firm will be far stronger for such co-operation, as it will tend to more harmonious working. The workpeople are bound to realise that only the best results can be obtained by the closest co-operation and good fellowship, but of course I don't know how this magazine will be received by everybody. I should imagine that it will be adversely criticised, the idea will be laughed at by perhaps five per cent, but then I don't think this really matters; so long as we have ninety-five per cent the magazine will be a success, as we shall do our best to see that it provides interesting reading to every member of the firm.

No member can fail to realise the position that this firm holds in the printing world in this country, especially when some of them look back to twenty years ago when it was a little jobbing place doing the sloppiest theatrical printing that was ever printed; and perhaps it would be interesting to a good many of our readers to know what really did take place in the early stages. Such men as Mr Hird and Mr Hanson (who has just retired) have some idea, and perhaps it would be a good thing if I gave you a rough outline of the principal incidents which have led up to this magnificent organisation. According to hearsay (I say hearsay because I was not with the firm at the time), the firm of John Waddington was started from a hand cart with sundry quoins, type and chases, bought very cheaply, and dumped down in an office in Wade Lane.[1] This was the commencement of the firm. Wilson Barrett helped the late Mr John Waddington, and the office staff sat on soap boxes and ran round to the customers to get the money for the wages every week. Sometimes they got it, but not always. I cannot write with a definite certainty about the firm in these early stages, because I am only relying upon what I have been told; so we will be content to say that the firm started on nothing and did not really become a firm until it was turned into a Limited Liability Company in 1905, the premises then having been moved to Great Wilson Street.

I remember one night, I was then Lithographic Foreman at Harrison, Townsend and Co., and my brother-in-law (Mr Walter Turner of the artists' room) asked me if I would like a change. Being of an adventurous disposition, I instantly said 'Yes', because as a matter of fact I was fed up with the job I then held, so to cut a long story short, I saw Mr Waddington, and he engaged me as Lithographic Foreman over two machines at Great Wilson Street; and well do I remember the awful agony of the first two months. You see I was taking the place of the foreman who was dying of consumption, and he must have had a good many sympathisers because everything was done that was humanly possible, such as putting acid in water, removing screws from the machine, putting a tremendous amount of pressure on the cylinders and various other things too numerous to mention, in order to prevent me from making good, and it was only the fact that I had a twelve month agreement which enabled me to retain the position I held. However, things went along and we were doing nothing else but theatrical work. Sometimes the customers paid, more often they didn't. Of course we had our comedy, and I can well remember a man called Ginger (because he had a red head), who was foreman of the stone polishing department (himself

---

1 Quoins, type and chases are letterpress equipment; the chase is the frame within which the type in page format is secured by means of quoins which are expandable locking devices operated by means of a square ended tool.

and another), having a wrestling match with a man called Jasper who had a very large head. Ginger trained on port wine, which he used to obtain by singing comic songs in public houses. Jasper trained on beer, the only beverage he could afford. It was a proper match and was held during the dinner hour in the composing room, which was in the top storey of the building. They flew at each other like tigers, and it was with the greatest difficulty that the backers prevented both combatants from falling down the hoist. Ginger got the first fall, and in the second bout had Jasper face downwards on the floor with his arm under Jasper's face trying to turn him on his back. The silence was intense; nothing could be heard but the heavy breathing of the wrestlers, when suddenly Ginger gave a blood-curdling yell, screamed 'murder!', and they found Jasper had got his teeth in Ginger's forearm and the blood was pouring out as if he really had been murdered. The judges gave it out as a drawn match; it was the only safe thing to do.

We used to work very hard in those days, each man was doing his very best to keep the firm above water, but slowly and surely we were sinking. This was not because the workpeople were not doing their part: the office was wrong, the management was wrong, and we did not get paid for above half the work we turned out.

I will give you some more next month.

April 1927
Dear readers,

EVIDENTLY I WAS wrong when I stated in the last number that the magazine would be adversely criticised. If you remember, I said five per cent might criticise this first edition unfavourably, but this percentage has proved far too high, because really it has only represented one eighth per cent, so we need not trouble about this because we should feel very lonely if somebody did not oblige us.

I want to take the opportunity of thanking Mr Blades for the way in which he put the first number together, and when we consider the little material he had at his disposal, I think everybody will admit that as usual, I have been very lucky in finding the right man for the right job, and the fact that I have been lucky in finding right men has contributed largely to the success of the firm. It is evidently a gift which some men possess and some men do not, but it is absolutely essential that the heads of firms should have this gift if they are going to make a success of the business they are in control of, simply because the amount of work it is possible for one man to do (however clever he may be) is limited, therefore, unless he has very competent understudies (managers, foremen, sub-foremen, etc.) there must sooner or later come a time when the business will have reached its limits, and no business, however large, should ever reach its limits but must always keep expanding; there is no such thing as standing still, it must go forward or go backward.

But to resume the story of John Waddington Ltd. I said in the last issue that the firm did not become a firm until it was a Limited Liability Company in 1905. I understand that our present chairman, Sir Frederick Eley, (Bart), helped Mr John Waddington to form this company and supplied the wherewithal, so you will see that our chairman has been connected with this firm even longer than Mr R. B. Stephens and myself, although he did not take an active interest in it until later, when he became chairman. However, the fact that the company was formed did not stop the steady drift downhill, and the capital gradually disappeared. Mr R. B. Stephens, our present joint managing director, joined the Board in 1908; certain alterations were made, but although turnover increased by thirty-three per cent from that date until 1913 (when Mr John Waddington resigned) the difficulties of the company were as great, if not greater, than ever. It then became a question of selling up the place or economising in every direction, cutting down expenses, eliminating waste, avoiding bad debts, etc., and trying to preserve what little good trade we had in order that we might carry on. I have to be very careful here, because this is where I really come in and I would not like to take more than my share of the glory, so if I use the personal pronoun a little too much, I ask the indulgence of my co-directors in advance.

It was a pretty sorry job that was given to me because we had to commence to clean the copy book. A good many of its pages were dirty and, as I said before, we were doing the worst work in the country, and this had to be lived down; so we had to clean the copy book before we could have a clean start. Unfortunately, many of the workpeople had to be dispensed with, but still, in cases like these, I am sure you will agree with me that it is impossible to stand on sentiment. If we had adopted the latter course, everybody connected with the firm would have been out of work within a few months.

Our turnover at that time was £16,000 per annum, out of which several thousand pounds were written off as bad debts, so we had to get new business. I, personally, don't know how it was done, but it was done and things began to improve. Everybody in the firm at that time seemed to realise the difficult time we were passing through and did everything humanly possible to help. Early in January of the following year, we extended the

Elland Road factory and took out the Quad Crown litho. machines and put in 60 x 40s. This enabled us to compete for commercial posters and eliminated a lot of the risk attached to the highly speculative theatrical work. Things went merrily along and we were picking up rapidly until August 1914, when the war broke out and we were compelled to put all the staff on two-thirds pay as a precautionary measure, but after a few weeks we found out that it did not cripple us so much as we anticipated, and the firm paid back the money which had been withheld from the staff; as a matter of fact, we really did not feel the effect of the war for some months.

The next event of real interest happened on the night between 31 March and 1 April 1915, when the Elland Road factory was burned to the ground. I was awakened at half-past four in the morning by a loud knocking at the front door. Being April Fool's Day, I thought it was somebody playing a practical joke, and also as it was Good Friday, it might have been somebody selling hot cross buns; but as the knocking continued, I went down to the front door in my pyjamas and beheld our old friend Bob Slater, and the following conversation took place:

Myself: 'What's the matter, Bob?'
Bob: 'There's been a fire, sir.'
Myself: 'Great Wilson Street?'
Bob: 'No sir, Elland Road.'
Myself: 'Is it serious, Bob?'
Bob: 'No sir, not very, the roof's fallen in.'

We have all heard how Mr Edison, when seeing his factory in full blaze, gave instructions for the architects to get on with the plans for a new factory. This action was put down as being typically American, but next month I will tell you how Mr Stephens and myself tackled the situation and had the whole staff working in another factory within twenty-four hours, while the old factory was still smouldering.

May 1927
Dear readers,

THE SECOND NUMBER of the magazine, in my opinion, shows a marked improvement on the first, and if we carry on improving at this rate, the magazine will be something to be proud of in, shall we say, twelve months time. I personally feel sure that it is doing the work it was intended that it should do, viz. to bring all of us closer together; and before passing on to the story, I must again thank Mr Blades for the admirable work he is doing.

When I left off last month, I had just finished a very cryptic conversation with Bob Slater, and you all know how gently he broke the sad news to me.

The police had lent him a bicycle; Bob promptly handed this machine over to me, so that I could get on the scene of action without any delay. In passing, however, I must mention that this particular machine was made for a giant, and I could only touch the pedals when they came up to the top. However, as it was all downhill from Woodhouse Moor, I got over this difficulty, called in at the police station at Meadow Lane, and took the tramcar to Elland Road, accompanied by a lot of munition lady workers. They were discussing the fire, and expressing their delight that it had happened, because evidently it was a fine sight.

Bob was perfectly right; the roof had gone in, and the second floor also. There was nothing left but the four walls.

I had to go with a policeman to another police station. It was a beautiful morning; the sun was shining brilliantly; the policeman alluded to it, otherwise I should not have noticed, because I thought the end of the world had come. One seems so helpless when they are by themselves, and I wanted a lot of people round me so that we could get busy: so, I wired for Mr Spink from Thorpe Arch, sent for Miss Greig, called for Mr Turner and Mr Dixon, and then went up to tell Mr Stephens the bad news. Mr Stephens quite naturally was in bed, and it seemed to me to be ridiculous for anybody to be in bed when things like these were happening. I didn't realise it was only twenty past six in the morning. However Mr Stephens was soon down, and I said to him, 'Something very serious has happened – Elland Road is burned to the ground.' I thought he would be knocked into a heap the same as I had been – not a bit of it. He just calmly said, 'All right, let's have some breakfast!'

About ten o'clock in the morning I heard that the late Charles Russell's business was for sale, and Mr Stephens and myself got into touch with his executors.

I had previously told all the lithographers that they would be put on half salaries, and to report at nine o'clock every morning, because it was absolutely necessary to keep the staff together.

By twelve o'clock tentative arrangements had been made to purchase the late Mr Russell's business, and Mr Stephens and myself went over to Harrogate during the afternoon to conclude the transaction, and we got permission to commence working on Saturday morning: so when the lithographers turned up as arranged at nine o'clock on the Saturday morning, they were promptly taken round to Union Mills and they manned the machines and started reprinting what had been burned. We worked all Saturday, Sunday, Easter Monday and Tuesday. Everybody worked with a will. They evidently realised that the position was very serious, and I cannot praise this 'Old Guard' sufficiently for the work that they did on that occasion. It was all very trying, but trying times like these have their uses, because they bring out the best in every man and woman. It also showed me a new Mr Stephens. I did not know him as well then as I do now. The calm, cool manner in which he dealt with this difficult position gave me the confidence and the support which I needed so very badly on that occasion, and I must say that I alone could not have done one-tenth of what was actually done with Mr Stephens' co-operation. He supplied what I had not got, because you must bear in mind that I was not so accustomed to handle the intricacies of business then as I am today: therefore I should have been unable to cope with the many difficult propositions that presented themselves at that time.

We have now arrived at the Wednesday morning after the holidays, and here a very strange thing occurred, because all the late Mr Charles Russell's workpeople came in, and not one of them had heard that there had been a fire, and to see the look of blank dismay on their faces when they saw their machines manned by strangers, was really an education. It was on this occasion that I first met Mr Cameron, and I must say that I had not the slightest idea at that moment that he would play such an important part in the success of the firm, although I did single him out at that time for a position in the future, and of course Mr Cameron was one of the entire staff which we took over from the Russell business, so you will see nobody was thrown out of employment.

Well, in two or three months we had got Union Mills in something like order. We had replaced the printing which it was necessary to replace, and notwithstanding the fact that every week some important employee was called to the Colours, still this did not prevent the firm from pushing ahead.

As you know, all our business was theatrical printing at that time, and in order that we should be in touch with the proprietors of shows when they were produced in London, I had for a long time been considering the necessity of actually printing in London so that we could get the work for the various tours, and therefore the idea of a small London factory got bigger and bigger in the minds of Mr Stephens and myself, as we could both see how very necessary this was. So I was instructed by the Board to get ahead with the scheme. Every master printer in Leeds to whom I mentioned it, said that I was mad to entertain the idea.

Next month I will tell you how it was done.

June 1927
Dear readers,

THE BOARD (Mr Edgar Lupton, chairman), having definitely decided on the policy of having a works in London, it was left to me to find suitable premises, which was rather a tall order, because it was essential to have the works right in the middle of Theatreland; however, my usual luck came to my assistance, and I had my attention drawn to a small three-storied building in a yard in Floral Street, which could be adapted and made suitable if various alterations were made. A lease for twenty-one years was entered into between ourselves and the landlord. The machinery had now to be installed, and although we had made considerable headway since February 1913, still, money was not plentiful, and the strictest economy had to be used in every direction. I bought one or two machines from Messrs Goodall and Suddick, who were giving up business, and bought the remainder from a firm in Covent Garden called Ballantyne, Hanson and Co. These people used to do all the publishing for Sir Walter Scott. There was one item of furniture I would have liked very much to have bought, and that was a chair that Sir Walter Scott used to sit in to correct his proofs. This sold for a very big figure, and of course such things were out of my line altogether.

Mr Heseldine, who was foreman of the poster department in Great Wilson Street, accepted the position of manager, and Mr Bowers was the representative. The first man I engaged in London was Mr Fred King, as foreman compositor, who remained with us for some ten years and then left to join Messrs David Allen. I always thought a good deal of Mr King; he was a most conscientious worker, and naturally I was sorry to lose him, because one hates to lose old comrades who have helped in the building up of this big business.

It was a tall order to obtain the printing for the West End theatres of London, because these people are very conservative, had made friends with their printers and kept friendly for years; but just at that time, Messrs David Allen sold their Wealdstone factory to the Government, which left the field open for John Waddington Ltd, and they did not fail to take full advantage of the opportunity presented, and with the introduction of two-colour type (which was new for theatrical printing in those days) we soon made a clean sweep of practically the whole of the West End theatre business, and as we did the printing for the opening dates, we were in touch with the people who took the shows out on tour consequently, so we obtained the printing for the tours, whereas before the introduction of the London premises, we used to get into touch with them when all their arrangements had been made.

Prices were very high at that time, and I must say that it was not altogether energy and brains which made Floral Street a success, because a combination of circumstances favourable to the venture helped to bring about the desired results. Of course, Floral Street would have been of very little use if it had not been for the support given to it by the Leeds works. The lithographic and letterpress work too big for Floral Street to tackle used to come up one day and the printing was sent down the next day; this was done on many an occasion – in fact the whole firm entered whole-heartedly into the business in order to give this small concern every possible chance – so the credit is not due to Floral Street alone, but to the firm, although a considerable amount is due to the help they obtained from Leeds, and things went merrily along. Everybody connected with the firm appeared to be perfectly happy and comfortable, which proves that hard work need not necessarily make people unhappy, and in fact as a rule tends to make them contented and generally pleased with life, appreciating to the fullest extent their few hours of recreation.

Nothing really of great interest now happened for some considerable time. We have got to 1916, and the war, as you know, was playing havoc, and we could not see very far ahead. What with government restrictions and the men being called to the front, business, although there was plenty of it, became increasingly difficult. A large amount of my time was spent on the Advisory Board and Tribunals, and I travelled to London and back once every week, catching the midnight train up to London on the Monday night, and the midnight train on the Thursday night back again. This was necessary, because all the managers had been called to the Front. A man could make his arrangements and adopt a policy one day, only to find when he opened his newspaper next morning that certain government regulations had made all his arrangements abortive. The restrictions to bill-posting were one of the biggest set-backs we had. We had purchased a large amount of paper, trying to foresee everything, and then the Government said that nothing bigger than a double crown could be posted on the hoardings; consequently the price of MG paper came tumbling down, and we had to sell our stocks in order to save as much as possible from the wreck. No sooner had this stock been released than the Government reversed its decision instead – a four-sheet could be used – and this decision remained in operation until after the War, but then we had no paper.[2]

---

2 Crown was a paper size 15 inches x 20 inches – hence double crown was 20 inches x 30 inches. MG meant 'machine glazed' and was a type of paper for posters. A four sheet poster was made up of four sheets, each sheet being 60 inches x 40 inches.

So you will see although orders were easy to obtain, still they were very difficult to execute, what with the lack of material and the lack of experienced workmen.

These circumstances did not, however, prevent the policy of forging ahead, and in 1918 arrangements were practically complete to purchase the Stoke Newington factory, but owing to the fact that the Germans pushed our troops back in France a considerable distance, we did not think it safe to go forward with the venture, and therefore this matter was shelved and only taken up again when the war came to an end.

I will continue next month.

July 1927
Dear readers,

I NOW PASS on to Armistice Day, when hostilities ceased, and we that were left of John Waddington Ltd could hardly realise that the war was over. I think we all seemed to wake up out of some horrible dream. Trade was good, the troops were commencing to come over in thousands, and had money to burn. Consequently, the theatrical business flourished for some two years, and although we set on every man as soon as he was released still we could not cope with the work we had to execute. I might state here that although practically three staffs went to the Front from John Waddington Ltd, a sum total of between 160 and 170, and the number of employees before the war was only about sixty, still we absorbed every man as he was released.

It was in January 1919 when negotiations were resumed to purchase the Stoke Newington factory, and everything was carried through satisfactorily to all parties. Sir Frederick Eley (who had resigned his position as general manager of the National Provincial Bank) was asked to become chairman, and Mr Lupton who was chairman and who for many years had given the firm the benefit of his calm and sound advice, vacated the chair for Sir Frederick, knowing that Sir Frederick's influence would be of great assistance to the firm in the near future. The Board was then composed as follows: Sir Frederick Eley, chairman; Mr Edgar Lupton, vice-chairman; Mr Arthur Copson-Peake (now Sir Arthur Copson-Peake); Mr R. B. Stephens, and myself.

The Stoke Newington factory which we had purchased as a printing factory was about the biggest mess I had seen in my life. The type was old and battered, and the machinery almost as bad as the type; the whole place was run by two gas engines placed in the centre of the factory, taking up nearly as much room as all the machinery; the building was lighted by gas;

no attempt had been made to keep the place tidy, and everything was conducted in the most slovenly manner imaginable. The first thing that was done was to cut off the gas and install electricity; we then took out the gas engines and ran by motor power, bought new type, and did everything funds would allow in order to make this factory turn out work equal to the Waddington standard.

Things did not go very well at first, simply because the workpeople did not know the management. You see they had just become part of the firm, and we can forgive them for not knowing that the Board was always generous, just and courteous. Now we know the Stoke Newington branch is fully as loyal as any of the other factories, and is, without doubt, the more consistently successful branch.

August 1927
Dear readers,

CONTINUING FROM LAST month, I said Stoke Newington had just become part of the firm. At this period, Mr Spink went down to put the house in order, and with typical cockney wit they christened him 'The Silent Menace'.

Ninety-four per cent of the work done at this time by Stoke Newington was done for one customer, the London Theatre Varieties. We had not had the factory long before we were threatened with the loss of this contract, and I want you to realise our position when we were faced with this contingency; if the contract had gone at that time, we should have had a works and no work to do. However, we got over the difficulty and a satisfactory agreement was made whereby such a state of affairs could not occur again; but it was a severe lesson for us, and we therefore set about getting new customers and still retaining the old, so that it was not very long before the ninety-four per cent became fifty per cent and then twenty-five per cent, and now Stoke Newington has its own customers and is not dependent upon any one customer – which, of course, is a healthy state for any firm to be in.

I must here (although he is my brother), pay a great compliment to the untiring efforts of Mr Horace Watson. He is a man about whom Leeds knows very little. He has taken the full responsibility on his own shoulders, which relieves me very considerably, and makes my work much lighter, because for the past five years I have not visited Stoke Newington more than five times, and if we had had a manager at Stoke Newington who had to be constantly overlooked, it would have been impossible for us to have advanced in other directions, because Stoke Newington would have taken up too much time. Stoke Newington is one of the tightest businesses imaginable, as Mr Horace uses the strictest economy, and also strives, at the same time, after efficiency. They have now much more up-to-date machinery, and although it is not our intention to ever do the highest class of printing, still, they must keep up-to-date. So good luck to the Stoke Newington branch.

September 1927
Dear readers,

The next venture John Waddington Ltd embarked upon was the purchase of the mother company, Waddingtons Ltd, of Camp Road. As the old printers of Leeds know, the late Mr John Waddington went into a kind of partnership with the late Mr Wilson Barrett, and for some years carried on a printing business under the name of Waddingtons Ltd. Mr Ben Roberts was chairman of that company, and he evidently disagreed with Mr Waddington, and the latter left and began business on his own account, and thus started the firm which, as I have previously stated, afterwards became John Waddington Ltd.

The child of the mother company by this time had grown so very big that the mother was only a very small old lady, but still, this old lady had very influential friends, such as Mr John Hart, and Howard and Wyndhams, and therefore in 1919, Mr R. B. Stephens entered into negotiations with Mr Ben Roberts to purchase the whole of the business of Waddingtons Ltd, lock, stock and barrel. These negotiations were completed, and Waddingtons Ltd was run as a separate company, and Mr Stephens and myself were elected directors, along with Mr John Hart, Mr Walter Roberts, Mr Roberts and Mr Ledgard.

Waddingtons Ltd were losing at least £50 per week when we took this firm over, and this loss was very quickly turned into a profit and the workpeople were much better off by the change. The policy we adopted was to reduce the prices and get more output from the factory, and consequently the overhead charges were automatically reduced. The policy which had been pursued prior to the purchase had been high prices and little work turned out; consequently, the higher the prices were, the fewer were the orders that came into the factory, and the position got worse and worse, until, as I have stated, we obtained control.

There were extenuating circumstances for the loss which I say Waddingtons Ltd was incurring. Mr Drakeford had been called to the Colours, and could not, while he was away, give it the attention that is necessary for a printing house; consequently a lot of their customers left them, and everybody knows the difficulty in which a firm is placed when it loses customers, because the new customers which are obtained are not the same as the old. Personally, I would rather retain one good customer than get three new ones, because out of the three new customers, possibly only one is retained, and then that one might not be as good as an old customer with whom you may have been doing business for years, knowing his requirements and he knowing your capabilities.

October 1927
Dear readers,

THE WORKS OF Waddingtons Ltd were badly designed; the whole thing was badly arranged. The composing room was on the fourth storey, up very steep steps, and every forme had to go down to the machine room in the basement. I have often sympathised with the manager there for with every small order that came in, this poor fellow had to walk up those steps or get somebody to break off his work and see him, and to go up and down eight or ten times a day was misapplied energy. So we let the fourth storey, sold the obsolete litho. plant, put the compositors on the ground floor, economised in many other directions, and turned a loss into a profit. Things then went on smoothly there (under Mr Drakeford's management) right up to the time of getting into Wakefield Road, when all the odds and ends of places were amalgamated under one big roof. But before this time had arrived, the Board of Waddingtons Ltd had dissolved, and the business came under the direct control of the principal Board of John Waddington Ltd, and the old directors of Waddingtons Ltd, Camp Road, were very well satisfied at the way things had turned out.

In the meantime, we had rented a big stock room at Hope Mills because we had no place to keep our stock; we had also got a garage; Mr Vauvelle had come to us, a separate photographic establishment. So you can see, before we came to Wakefield Road, we had Union Mills, Dewsbury Road; Waddingtons Ltd, Camp Road; Hope Mills, Water Lane; Mr Vauvelle, photographic department, closely associated with us; a garage in Great Wilson Street, and also our head office in Great Wilson Street. So the time had now arrived when it was absolutely essential to bring all these various warehouses, businesses, etc. under one roof, and therefore, with this aim in view, land was purchased in Dewsbury Road, near Middleton Park, with a view to building a model factory.

The plans were all completed, and even the quantities sent out and everything approved by the Board, when it was brought to the notice of the directors that the factory we now occupy was vacant and would be sold; so weighing everything in the balance, and taking into consideration the tremendous costs of building at that time (they have since been considerably reduced), we thought it would be better, although we had bought the land, not to build on it; and it was arranged to approach the Conqueror Typewriter people and ascertain if these works could be purchased at a reasonable figure. (To be continued.)

January 1928
Dear readers,

WE HAD SCARCELY got into Wakefield Road when we found it was necessary to put on a new roof. This fact was accepted philosophically, simply because I personally had had so much tinkering about with old factories that I should have felt at a loose end if something like this had not occurred – the disease had become a habit with me. So, first of all, we plastered the roof with bitumastic, spending about £700, only to find that it was useless, and there was nothing left but to spend several thousands and put a new roof over the entire building simply because some fathead had built the factory on American lines, and considered it to be a steel building; I always called it tin, and nobody in their proper senses would have ever put up such a factory and such an expensive one to maintain. Thank heaven we have brick at both ends and a substantial roof, and the sooner we get a brick wall on both sides, the better.

I had often looked with envy upon the efforts made by large firms in order that better conditions for employees should prevail. I had looked with longing eyes upon such firms as Messrs Reckitt, Messrs Lever Bros. and Messrs Bryant and May. I say looked with envy, not that I wanted to take away the advantages from their employees, but to do something on similar lines for John Waddington Ltd; therefore, as soon as ever the question of new premises was discussed, provisions were made for sufficient land to be purchased in order that recreation grounds could be provided.

I never thought, even with the assistance of my rather vivid imagination, that John Waddington Ltd would be able to do what has been done for their workpeople as regards recreation.

I instantly approached my co-directors, and they gave me their whole-hearted support and furnished round about a thousand pounds for the fitting up of the various sports grounds.

February 1928
Dear readers,

LAST MONTH I told you that the directors kindly furnished round about a thousand pounds towards the sports grounds, and I must say efforts were not, at first, appreciated to the full. There were, however, extenuating circumstances. In the old place, the men and women had not had an opportunity of taking part in games, and had been compelled to form other habits of life, and I soon knew that I should have to be patient before the workpeople realised their real good fortune; so although the efforts of the Board as regards recreation were not taken up immediately, still, we had to keep a smiling face, knowing that everything would be right.

I am happy to say, now, that the recreation side of the business is fully appreciated by every member of the firm, and everything is going well in this direction. Both the cricket and the football clubs have won cups, and there is a feeling that the directors have all along striven not for themselves, but for their workpeople and staff.

The canteen was one of our biggest worries. Nothing seemed to go right and although we genuinely did our best, still, it is very difficult to satisfy so many people all having different tastes. Even a mother of a large family experiences this difficulty, because Willie likes some things and Mollie likes other things, and unfortunately, although we were prepared to contribute very considerably towards the canteen, still, we could not get the workpeople sufficiently interested even to form a committee and run the whole canteen themselves; but however, things are going much better now.

The heating of the premises caused us a lot of worry – in fact they have all been worries. We found that we were burning forty tons of coal per week. Just think of it; that awful boiler was like a prehistoric monster devouring everything, not only the profit that should have been ours, but some of the capital. (We have just sold it for £120. Thank Heaven.)

When we took these premises we thought we had any amount of room, and the general opinion among printers was that we had got a barracks, and no machines to fill it. We soon, however, had to build a large warehouse at the back. Bang went another £3,000. An enlargement of Mr Vauvelle's studio, another little bit on the playing card side – Oh! what a worry it has been.

March 1928
Dear readers,

LAST MONTH I told you that the heating apparatus had all to be revised in order to enable us to do without that prehistoric monster. Now I think we are about right for five minutes at any rate, although I am just thinking of putting two more bays on the south side of the building. It is wonderful how you say to yourself, 'Now we have finished, no more expense,' and the next morning you wake up with a brainy idea, and all your good resolutions go to the wind.

Well, to resume the story. I am now approaching a subject I must allude to, because this history of the firm would not be complete unless I alluded to the General Strike; but before doing so, I would like to recall another strike we had.

I know this is going back over the ground I have already traversed, but perhaps you will forgive me for recalling some very amusing incidents.

There was a proper, genuine strike between the Trades Unions and the Master Printers' Federation. We had to stand by our guns in just the same way as the members of the Trades Unions had to stand by theirs, and both parties decided to fight.

Having a dated printing business, of course it was very awkward for us, and we had to attempt to carry on at all costs – the litho. department, of course, could remain idle. So I got round me in London some seven or eight compositors and machine men and brought them up as blacklegs in order to try to fulfil the dated printing which was necessary for our customers, and I remember a certain night when it seemed to me that thousands of people in Great Wilson Street were waiting for these blacklegs to appear. I was standing in my office, looking down on this very orderly and smiling assembly, wondering how I should get these blacklegs home. All the front was securely guarded, no breach could be made in the enemy's ranks whatever. Of course I knew that no violence would be exercised, but still, I wanted to retain the services of the blacklegs, because we wanted to preserve the business for when our workmen returned.

How was I to get them out of Great Wilson Street unmolested? The back entrance ran straight into Water Lane, but there was a wall which surrounded a graveyard. It was summer, about ten o'clock, and dusk had set in, so I led my gallant henchmen through the graveyard, and we suddenly appeared out of the gloom in front of the old gravedigger, who was trimming up the gardens. I only wish you could have seen the expression on this gravedigger's face. He thought all the ghosts had come to frighten him to death. He dropped his shovel, glared, and when he got his speech back, he asked, 'Who are you – where are you going? You cannot go through here.' I opened my mouth and he knew then that we were mortal, and everything was all right, but still, he absolutely refused to give us permission to go through the graveyard, through his house, and so to safety.

After a good deal of argument I espied his 'missus', and I must say that I have always had more success with women than with men. I explained the position to her, she blackguarded her husband, took us through the house, and Mr Musgrave of the Typographical Society was for the time being beaten, and Victor Watson was triumphant.

However, we got another day's work out of these men the next day, but in the meantime Mr Musgrave had found out where they were lodged, which was the Golden Lion Hotel (at which our Leeds men have held many social gatherings), and I was surprised the following night not to see a soul, and going down to the works next morning, very early, no blacklegs appeared. Mr Musgrave had interviewed these men, paid their fares back to London, seen them on the train himself, and consequently honours were even. We had both scored a point, and since that time I have shaken hands with Mr Musgrave and laughed at the incident. Everything was fair and above board from the very commencement to the signing of the peace, which happened two or three days later.

The foregoing was a genuine, honest, straightforward battle between employer and employee; there was not the slightest feeling of animosity exhibited on either side; each one was doing his best, and there is nothing I like to meet better in life than a good competitor and a good friend.

April 1928
Dear readers,

LAST MONTH I told you some incidents about the Printers' Strike, and now I have to tell about a far different one – the General Strike of 1926.

I remember on a certain Monday night I had for the first time realised that a general strike throughout the whole country was imminent, because I never for a moment imagined that Britishers would allow the Bolshies to have their own way to such a degree, and I delivered a speech in the canteen, when I did my best to prevent my greatest friends (the employees) making a huge mistake. I pleaded with them, I pointed out the advantages of being members of the greatest empire that has ever existed, and so forth, but still all my efforts were unavailing. However, we will let that pass.

We will now come to the battle, and I want you to treat this matter in the same jocular vein that I feel at present. Again it was a fight, but unfortunately a fight which neither the employers nor the employees of John Waddington Ltd had any chance whatever to alter. The men went out, certain non-union people remained in, and now I think of the situation quietly, I seem to see close on 2,000 people outside the gates, howling and screaming because we tried to carry on.

Beds were ordered, sent for, and obtained, and we did our best to carry on, in the interests of this glorious Empire and for the Empire only (this is the team spirit that is talking now, boys, the team spirit). I don't wish to hurt anybody's feelings because it is finished and done with, but I must tell the history of the firm, and cannot let this incident pass because it made such a big impression on my mind, and involved such a serious loss to the firm.

I might say here that for every pound's worth of printing we sent out, it cost us £4 or possibly more. I have never been able to find out exactly how much this particular strike did cost the firm.

I am only, however, alluding to the amusing incidents. Of course, as you all know, we were isolated. I slept on my office desk along with Mr Norman, and I may say that oak is not conducive to sleep, especially when Mr Norman's arms went out as if he was fighting Bolshies, and all that sort of thing, and I had to keep one eye on his arm all the night and get what rest I could with the other eye.

Then I remember another incident when patrolling the weak side in the encampment. I came across three men in the darkness. When I got near enough to see them, I found that these three men should have been in the canteen; instead of which they had been in some local pub. One man seemed to be sober, and the other two had been searching for strikers. They had met each other in the dark and sloshed each other and consequently the third man found one man on his back, and the other man standing over him. No doubt you have heard this story told in a more graphic way.

However, we kept the flag flying, and I say the flag because we literally, hoisted the Union Jack, which, I think, saved the situation. I have not gone into great detail here, only mentioned the amusing incidents, but Mr Stephens and myself realised that thousands of pounds were going out of the coffers and that we should have to work many, many months and perhaps years, to make up for the deficit. Think of this, seriously, everybody.

However, that is past history, and I am now approaching the present time.

Of course, you all know that the old building has recently been demolished. I am alluding to Great Wilson Street. I shall always remember the building in Great Wilson Street as the cradle of this very wonderful firm of ours. (I have been in the top storey when it has rocked just like a cradle.) Still, it served its purpose. It gave birth to the finest printing house in the north of England, to a great firm which is now only on the first rung of the ladder. It was the birthplace of finding employment for a thousand workpeople, all of whom, I hope, are happy, and who fully realise that the directors of this big firm have never lost sight of the comfort of the people who have served the firm faithfully.

But before I close this history, I should like to point out that we have during the last twelve months got palatial premises in Charing Cross Road, in keeping with the dignity and prestige of this big firm of ours.

This brings me to the conclusion of this story, which is by no means a complete history of John Waddington Ltd. I shall have to leave this in the hands of better men than myself, perhaps 200 years hence. I wonder what is in store for us, because even as I close this series of articles, bigger things are in the offing, large undertakings have to be grappled with in the immediate future, and I wonder what the size of John Waddington Ltd will be when ten more years have rolled by?

[End of Victor Watson's story up to 1926]

CHAPTER FOUR

A REMINISCENCE OF THE EARLY DAYS

BY VICTOR WATSON, WRITTEN IN 1928

I EXPECT GENERALLY, when a man sets out to make a success in life, he is prepared to do anything, go anywhere (and I was going to say, do anybody – but no, I never have been guilty of that) and speaking generally, if a man is prepared to do these things, as a rule he succeeds, and when success has been attained he can look back, in his quiet and leisure hours, on the things he has done, and wonder how it was possible for him to screw himself up to such a pitch as to be able to do them.

I can recall one instance quite clearly. It was in 1910. I was trying to keep the firm alive, under the late Mr John Waddington. I never missed an opportunity to bring business into the firm, and consequently, as we were doing practically all theatrical work at that time, I mixed with all classes of theatrical people. We used to do business with a man called George Street, who ran *The Cattle Thief*. This, as the title denotes, was a Western drama, and perhaps one of the very best of its kind that has ever been seen in this country. George Street was the only actor employed in the cast, and he used to pick any man up that he saw in the street that was down and out, teach him a few American sayings, show him how to fire a blank cartridge, and knock a few chairs and tables over, and instantly he produced a second Martin Harvey.[1] He used to line up all these actors when he had got them trained and scream to them at the top of his voice, 'Now, you line of Martin Harveys, what about it?' He had a nickname for each individual, such as 'Sloppy' and 'Pinky', and never referred to them by any other name than the one that had struck him as soon as ever he had engaged him.

---

1 Martin Harvey was a well known actor manager of the day.

We had done all the work for *The Cattle Thief*, and they had done big business, and one day we received a wire that Mr George Street wanted Victor Watson to go up to London to see him about a new production he was doing called *The Bad Man*, and stay the weekend with him. If I had known what a weekend it was going to be, I don't think that even I would have ventured on this journey.

Mr Waddington wanted to give me 30/- for expenses, but I pointed out to him that the fare to London and back was 30/-, so I got this increased to £3. I had to put a considerable amount of my own money to it (and I hadn't much in those days) and then I set off. Mr Street met me at King's Cross Station in a Ford car, and we journeyed out to Brixton, where he was rehearsing *The Bad Man* in the afternoons and playing *The Cattle Thief* at night. The day I arrived was Friday, and that evening's performance went off quite all right. After the show we started playing 'Banker' with Sloppy and Pinky. I was fortunate enough to win a few shillings; if it hadn't been for this I don't know what I should have done, as you will hear later.

On Saturday I got lost in London, as I had not taken a note of the lodgings, so I went to the theatre and ultimately found my bearings again, and having had practically nothing to eat, arrived at the theatre at six o'clock. At half-past six it was found that Pinky was down with pneumonia. As a matter of fact I don't think he had recovered from the night before. I noticed he was very drunk; at any rate, he couldn't play, so I was asked to take his part. I had seen *The Cattle Thief* many many times, so I agreed, and they promptly proceeded to make me up as a Mexican. They put on me a big sombrero, all silver. It weighed about a ton. I think it cost about $40, and the moustache that they stuck on me they could have tied at the back of my neck.

I have always considered that I was a handsome chap, but when I looked in the glass after they had finished operating, I thought that I was the worst thing that could possibly have been created. However, I don't wish to flatter myself in any way, but my debut as an actor was received with great enthusiasm at the Brixton Theatre. I remember one scene where myself, Sloppy and two other cowboys were supposed to be playing 'Nap' in a saloon, and I said to them, 'Let's play real Nap.' We got so absorbed in the game that George Street had to come and fire a pistol over the table to wake us up. However, I was highly commended for the performance, and then my troubles started.

The landlady where I was staying, thinking that I was going home that night, had let my room. I don't quite remember what all her suggestions were, because we had had one or two in the bar. Well, to cut a long story short, about half-past three in the morning I settled down in the kitchen on a couch. It was summer time, and I woke, I should say about half-past four, and the whole floor was covered with black beetles. Now, if there is one thing that I do hate, it is a black beetle. I daredn't get down, and I had to make as much noise as possible. I had nothing to throw at them, and I spent the remainder of that night gazing upon these horrible things. I say I had only had one or two, and they were black beetles and not green or pink. However, all things come to an end, and thank Heavens, that night came to an end.

We had now got to the Sunday morning, and I might say the landlady had two daughters. Had I known their drinking capacity I should never have had anything to do with them. They took me out on to Clapham Common to a little public house, and all they could drink were large brandies and sodas. My funds were running fairly low, so I had to say I had an appointment, or else I honestly believe they would have been there yet.

I then went on a jaunt into Surrey with George Street. He had a friend who was a police inspector, so we had afternoon tea, and everything was all right until they decided to show me round the house and grounds, including the prison cells. I had never been into a cell before, and had barely got inside when – clash! – the door closed behind me and they kept me there for two hours. Knowing my vocabulary, you can quite understand that the air was electrified on my release. We got back to London about ten o'clock at night and I don't think anybody will prevail upon me to visit a country constabulary station again.

I don't think I have mentioned the chauffeur before, but anyway, Ananias was George Washington's brother compared with this youth. He also was one of the actors. He used to act in his spare time, and he was just as mad on the stage as he was driving a motor car. He had run away from home the year before, at least, so he said, and as the company were travelling up north to Edinburgh, he asked permission to borrow the car in order to see his dear, dying mother that night. George replied, 'My boy, look after your mother, she is the best friend you will ever have', and tears came into all our eyes, mine included, because again I had had one or two, and one gets sentimental when one has had a few drinks – at least I do.

So we dropped George Street at his lodgings, and the chauffeur asked me if I minded accompanying him to see his dying mother. I said 'No, but I am very tired, hurry back as soon as ever you can.' 'Well,' he said, 'I am not going anywhere near there; in fact I haven't a mother, but I know where there is a decent pub.' Now I want you to realise that I had no idea of the address where I was staying, and I had to rely upon this man driving me home, and I insisted upon being driven home, but no, he would take me to this public house, and then the bands started again. I ultimately arrived in bed this time, at four o'clock in the morning.

However, I got the order for the plant of printing for *The Bad Man*, and I had done my job. After I had paid my bill I had 17/6 in my pocket on the Monday, out of which I had to pay for my fare back home, and although very tired and very dirty, I was comparatively happy. On going to the London office in Chandos Street about three o'clock, I found a telegram waiting for me from the Governor, telling me to remain over until the following day, as he had some very particular business he wished me to attend to. So I went into Lockhart's and spent 10*d*., which reduced this 17/6 to 16/8. I remember the amount very well, and walking along the Strand that night, wondering where to lay my weary head, I came upon what I thought to be a very economical hotel called the Strand Imperial, just opposite the Gaiety Theatre. I never pass this hotel now without thinking of the mental agony I endured that night.

I succeeded in getting a room, and being very dirty, I bathed and dressed, and did the best I could with myself and went down to the lounge, trying to make myself as small as possible, because I felt like nothing on earth. I pretended to be reading a paper. There were two gentlemen in the room. One was constantly alluding to his cousin the Governor of a Province in India, in the best Oxford style. I think the other fellow must have come from Cambridge, because he kept alluding to a brother of his who was Field Marshall or something like that, and I wondered what kind of a place I had blown into, and thinking of the 16/8 in my pocket, my heart failed me. I could scarcely breathe. I went outside and paced in front of that hotel for about an hour.

Screwing up enough courage to go to my bedroom I opened the door leading into it, and saw a beautiful sitting-room; they had evidently given me a full suite. I went to bed, but all night I was thinking about the bill the next morning, and the 16/8 I had in my pocket. I had had nothing to eat since the repast I have referred to, at Lockhart's, about four o'clock the day before, so about half-past six, I could endure it no longer. I got up and was fully dressed at seven, got hold of my bag, pretended to be in a desperate hurry, and said, 'Could you let me have my bill, Miss?'

'Won't you stay for breakfast, sir?'

'No I can't, I shall miss my train.'

'It's all ready, sir.'

'No, I can't have my breakfast this morning, so sorry. Give me my bill, will you please?'

I got the bill, paid it in a trance, came out and realised the position. The amount I paid was 5/6 for bed and breakfast and I hadn't had the blessed breakfast. I mentioned this matter to a friend and said, 'What would you have done?'

'Well,' he said, 'I should have gone back and said I had missed the train!'

John Waddington came up the next day and we did a big deal of business; he gave me some more money to get back home, and everything was quite all right. Mrs Watson never knew one half of what had transpired, and I have kept her in ignorance all these years. Perhaps when she reads this she'll say it is too late to reap up old things, and she'll let it pass. At least I hope so.

CHAPTER FIVE

A GRANDSON'S RECOLLECTIONS

In 1990 I wrote my 'Recollections of Childhood', and in the following chapter I have extracted from my 'Recollections' the parts which bear on my grandfather's life and character.

When my father was little the family lived in the Brudenells below Woodhouse Moor in Leeds. The houses were packed together in terraces, the poorest having only a front and no garden. Next came the through terrace houses and a step up from those were the ones with a bit of garden at the front. They all had outside toilets in those days and although flush toilets had arrived by my time, I remember using the old toilets on many occasions. Through the hole you could see the clinker that was put down to soak everything up. Every so often somebody from the local authority came with a cart to empty the closets. I remember they used to call them the midnight mechanics.

When Dad took me round to see the various places that they had lived in, he explained how each was a step up for the family as Grandad was promoted to foreman and manager and then to general manager. He also explained how different it was living in those places in the early part of the century. For a start it was much nearer to the outskirts of Leeds where the country began. There were more open spaces for playing in and there were hardly any cars roaring by so the children played out and were safe. The only real blot was the smoke, which I remember as being really hateful. (At age seventeen I joined the Smoke Abatement Society, an organisation which made a tremendous impact but which is now no longer needed and is forgotten.) The streets were also proper communities and it was a big advantage socially to have all the people living at street level. A tower block of flats built by the council in the sixties is only like a row of houses put on its side, but with the great disadvantage that the inmates don't get to know each other.

Although my grandfather's origins were lowly I know that his home always had books in it. He also learned to play cards and to appreciate music, so I suppose his family was lower middle class. As soon as he could afford it, he organised better education for his children. My father went to Leeds Grammar School. Muriel, his sister, went to Leeds Girls High School and Eric, for a reason I have never understood, went to Ilkley Grammar School, where he shone as a cricketer.

My mother had been very bright at school and had gone on a secretarial course. Her first job as Ruby Hawker was at Waddingtons, and she soon got promoted to be the managing director's secretary, and then married his son. I remember that my grandfather had a tremendous affection for my mother. Mind you, I suppose everybody did because she was one of those rare people with ability but without vanity, and a sense of responsibility coupled with a sense of fun. Her colleagues at Waddingtons were Fanny Gregg (later Spencer), Ivy Wigglesworth (later Hibbert) and Lottie Compston (later Barnard and then Wimble). They continued to be my mother's friends and we saw them often, although Aunt Lottie went off to South Africa.

We moved to Conisby Dene, our house in Horsforth, in the summer of 1931. Grandad and Granny were already there at Clare House, a four-square stone Victorian house with a monkey puzzle tree on the front lawn. The tree was in almost the correct place to be the wicket for cricket, a game which my grandfather adored and used to play with us. Grandad had a car and a chauffeur and a dog called Nero. I remember that the car had a thermometer on the top of the radiator and it once got too hot when we were going up Sutton Bank in North Yorkshire. The car would not go up in first gear so Daddy, who was driving, reversed up the hill and that got the radiator boiling. Great excitement! Granny was alarmed. Daddy enjoyed it.

We always claim that the first game of Monopoly in Britain was played at Conisby Dene. I think I remember it, but I've been told the story so many times that I'm not so sure. I do definitely remember playing the prototype of the game Buccaneer. It was called 'Pieces of Eight' and had brass strips fashioned into the shape of the figure '8' to simulate Spanish coins. I also remember 'Samlo', which was launched shortly before the war and then had to be withdrawn because of the paper shortage.

Beric and I were sometimes taken to the Wakefield Road works of Waddingtons where Daddy had an office in the middle of the works. (I know exactly where!) We loved to play with the fascinating things there.

And we sometimes went to the Keighley factory – the old mill behind the Crabtrees' Garage, which was part of Ondura Tyres. This part of the Waddingtons operation was called the Lamonby Manufacturing Company, to keep secret the fact that it contained the amazing new playing card process which Daddy had developed. The long web of playing cards went through the ceiling from top to bottom of the place, and we were all agog every time we saw it. I remember Fred Harrison very well from those early days. He was the manager of the factory for all of his working life.

Music was very much a part of our lives but radio and gramophones were comparatively new and there was no great awareness of the breadth and diversity of music. Dad played the piano by ear, which is one of life's greatest gifts in my opinion. Songs and pieces that he played spring readily to my mind. He was fond of Chopin's 'Polonaise in A major', and Fritz Kreisler's 'Liebeslied' and 'Liebesfreud'. I remember my young brother Beric learning to sing 'Little man you've had a busy day', and in fact one day we went down to a recording studio in Shaw Lane, Headingley, where Dad made a few records, one of which was Beric singing that song. I wonder what happened to those records. Songs like 'The Isle of Capri', 'Red sails in the sunset' and 'When the deep purple falls' were all the rage.

> When the deep purple falls
> Over sleepy garden walls
> And the stars begin to flicker in the sky
> Through the mists of a memory
> You wander back to me
> Breathing my name with a sigh

Those words, written by Peter de Rose in 1939, and the haunting melody made a great romantic impression on me, an eleven-year-old boy. But I still thought it very funny when Arthur Askey and Stinker Murdoch, in the radio show *Band Wagon*, bowdlerised the song to include such lines as 'sloppy garden walls'. Probably the most memorable song for me is 'Love's old sweet song'. My mother used to sing it to us and I particularly remember her singing it to me and Beric as we climbed up the cliff at Torquay one evening when we were very little. I always think of my mother when we sing, 'Just a song at twilight'.

I didn't hear jazz until after the war because it was not in evidence at home. Similarly classical or highbrow music was not played very much either, and my appreciation of it only began at Bootham School.

Walt Disney's marvellous film, *Fantasia*, probably did more to popularise highbrow music than anything else. I never hear 'The Sorcerer's Apprentice' by Paul Dukas without visualising Mickey Mouse as the overwhelmed apprentice.

Grandad loved John McCormack, Caruso and Richard Tauber, but the songs were not heavy. Gilbert and Sullivan were very popular with all the adults of course, and the musicals of the day provided popular hits. Waddingtons had begun as a printworks which produced programmes and posters for the theatre, and although the company was into folding cartons, paper labels, playing cards, puzzles and games by the 1930s, the connection with the theatre continued. Grandad had many friends in show business and related activities such as journalism, and as he regularly spent two or three nights a week in London, staying at the Waldorf, he must have seen all the shows. Beric and I were not really aware of them though.

We were, however, very much aware of certain radio programmes. *Band Wagon* was a great favourite. That must have been one of the very first of the *ITMA* type programmes. Tony Handley with *ITMA (It's That Man Again)* introduced us to what one might call recognition humour. The catchphrases were not especially clever or funny, but when they were used week after week they became delightful friends. They included, 'Can I do you now Sir?', 'I don't mind if I do' and 'I go, I come back', and you still hear people using them over forty-five years later.

The programme *In Town Tonight* was another favourite, with the signature tune being Eric Coates' 'Knightsbridge March'. You heard the noise of London's traffic and suddenly it all screeched to a halt and the announcer said, 'We bring London to a halt to give you *In Town Tonight*.' It was most dramatic. But we really spent very little time listening to records or the radio. The news was almost compulsory listening during the war and we (Grandad, Dad and I) often listened to *The Brains Trust*, but otherwise we were none of us very frequent adherents.

I don't remember much about social events except the wedding of Uncle Eric and Auntie Mick. The highlights were the cake being cut with the sword of Auntie Mick's father, Captain Jack Tebbs, and me having to have an aspirin because I had a headache. The Christmas festivities stick in my mind though. We always had Christmas dinner at Granny and Grandad's, with boards and tablecloths on the billiard table. It seemed huge to me, with lots of people around it, including Great Uncles Claude and Horace. After the meal we always had a fight throwing rolled up paper napkins and cracker paper. Then there would be games and singing. Grandad usually put on some sort of theatrical performance. He played the one string fiddle, Daddy the piano, and Mummy the violin and the harmonica, and Uncle Eric and Auntie Muriel had very good tenor and soprano voices. Added to that, Uncles Claude and Horace were full of fun and games and monologues, so the general effect on a small boy was quite overwhelming. I can't remember being involved at all.

Apart from the great fun of Christmas, I have other particularly special memories of Grandad. Daddy made a den for me and Beric in the trees just by the drive of Conisby Dene. Having stationed us in the trees with our Robin Hood and Little John outfits (made by Mummy), and with bows and arrows ready, Grandad was invited to come across. I remember him walking down the drive in his Homberg hat and how we tried with our arrows to hit the hat. He often wore a Homberg – a super hat which got a bad name because the Chicago gangsters wore it.

One day, as a lad of eleven or twelve, with Beric and Billy Mason and some others, I was playing in the fields to the south of Scotland Lane, up towards Owlet Grange where Everard Chadwick lived later on.[1] Out of devilment we threw some old logs over the wall of the house when suddenly the upstairs window opened and a lady shouted at us. I shouted back cheekily as we ran off. A few days later I was at Clare House and Grandad said that a lady from up Scotland Lane had seen some boys misbehaving and being cheeky, and she thought that I was the ringleader. He asked if it was me. I said it wasn't. 'Oh, I'm glad about that', said Grandad, 'I'll tell her that it wasn't you.' Well of course he knew it was me. By believing me he made me feel terrible. I'd lied and yet been trusted. His wise handling of that affair made a deep impression on me and instilled a determination in me not to betray trust.

When I was about fourteen I was at Clare House one day when the vicar, The Reverend Wareham, had called. Grandad said 'Victor, the vicar thinks that it is time for you to be confirmed.' I said that I would rather wait until I was sure in my own mind, and Grandad wholeheartedly supported me in that attitude and the vicar was put off. We often used to have discussions on life, the universe and philosophical matters generally. I loved to be involved with Dad and Grandad and friends like Harold Beasley, and I was thoroughly irritated by people who could not think logically and either could not or would not talk about serious things. For example, when I said that I was an atheist and I didn't believe in heaven and hell, a lady asked me why I didn't go round killing people, as if the only reason for good behaviour was to

---

1 Everard Chadwick was a noted lawyer and became the chairman of Waddingtons.

avoid perdition. Such arguments were common in my young days and I was exasperated by them.

My grandfather was passionately fond of cricket and continued playing for a long time. I can remember him in a game at the Wakefield Road works ground, so he must have been over fifty then. It sticks in my mind because he received a nasty blow while fielding close in and I remember him being laid out on the field between the pavilion and the wicket, with everybody fussing round and some blood running from his nose. I have two wonderful cricketing souvenirs. One is a beautifully prepared book commemorating Grandad's time with the Headingley Cricket Club. The other is the autographed bat that he gave me. It has the signatures of the England and Australia Test Teams of 1929 and 1934.

During the autumn term of 1943 at Bootham I'd played a lot of chess, and as soon as I got home from school I challenged Dad and gave him a good game. In one term I'd improved enormously and one of Dad's great disappointments was that he never had the opportunity to pit me against Grandad. We played chess a great deal. Often at Clare House the game would continue during the meal, much to the annoyance of Granny and Mum. But Grandad and Dad and Uncle Eric said that chess was the game of the great generals and leaders and was more important than food. So Grandad, who left school at twelve, loved music, was widely read, played chess and bridge and became one of Leeds' most successful entrepreneurs.

VICTOR WATSON

Top left: John Waddington.

Top right: Victor Watson in 1935.

Right: Victor Watson aged thirty-five.

Top: The playing card factory at Keighley.

Left: Victor Watson at his desk in 1938.

Below: R. B. Stephens, chairman of Waddingtons, with HRH Princess Royal and Ernest Clegg, who designed the set of presentation county maps.

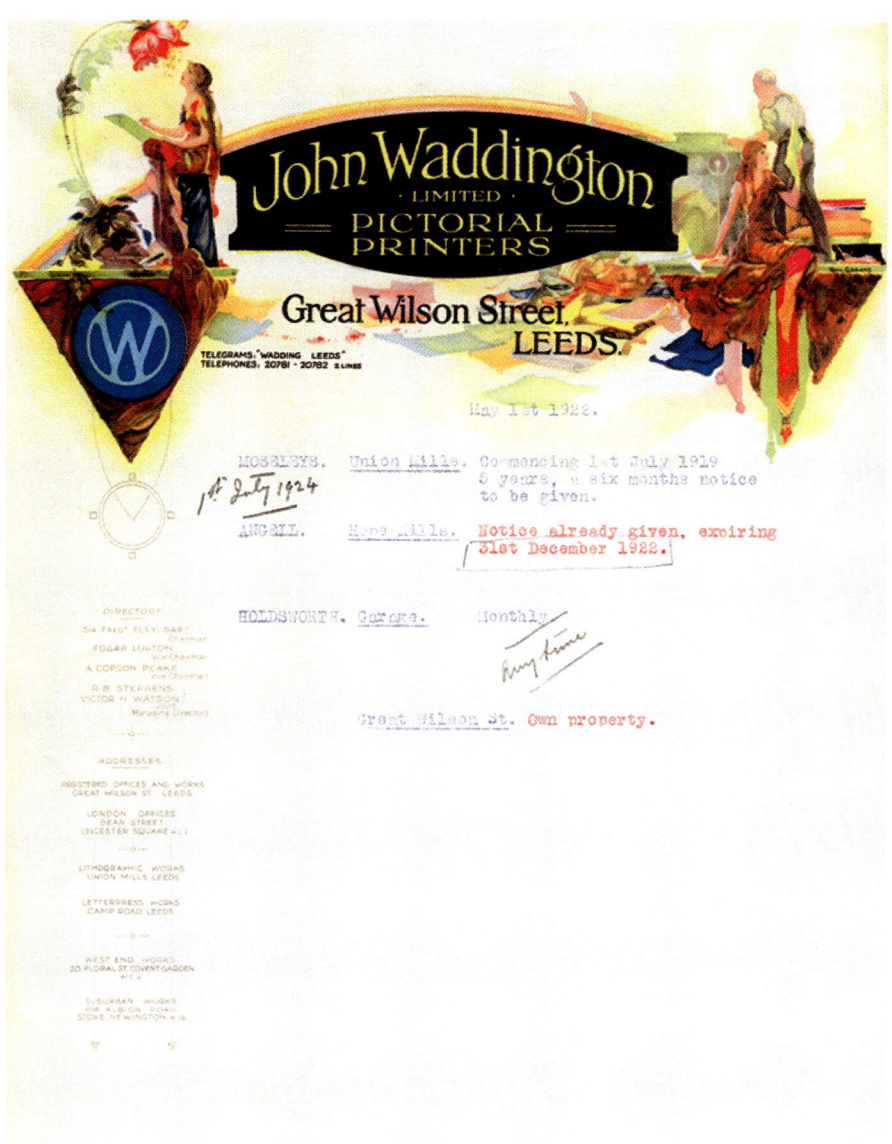

A letter heading of the 1920s used for special purposes to illustrate colour printing and the impact of flamboyant design.

CHAPTER SIX

LITHOGRAPHY AND COLOUR SEPARATION

As with many other successful businessmen, Victor Watson had just the right training and knowledge to exploit a new and growing sphere of technical progress. In addition to his expertise, he had abundant energy, the determination to succeed and that most useful ability to see a trend and take advantage of it.

He was a lithographer at a time when great improvements in colour printing were taking place. When I say 'colour printing', I mean the accurate depiction of a full colour subject and not just the earlier system of line printing with solid colour or tints added. The latter method was what existed until J. C. Le Blon, a German of French extraction, invented colour separation. In the early 1700s he produced the first mezzotints. This process entailed colour separation by hand and eye. The artist prepared a key drawing of the colour subject and then prepared printing plates for each of the three primary colours, yellow, red and blue, to be superimposed by successive printings. Le Blon also thought of adding the fourth colour of black to improve dark and shaded parts of the picture. Nowadays, instead of yellow, red and blue we use the complementary colours, a warmer yellow, cyan and magenta. Also, we use photographically generated dots of different sizes to make up each plate and provide the variation in colour. In Le Blon's day, it was a case of engraving a copper plate with a stippling tool and then altering the surface with a stylus, or flattening tool, to provide varying hollows on that surface, which was then inked and transferred to the paper or parchment on a hand press.

The idea of reproducing a picture in full colour by printing in four separate colours was a remarkable invention, but the method used was slow and expensive, so it was not commercially viable. However, in 1796, Alois

Senefelder invented lithography. He noticed that the Kelheim limestone which he was using for grinding ink accepted writing in greasy ink, and that the inked part of the stone repelled water when it was wetted, while the un-inked part accepted the water. When an inked roller or hand piece was applied to the stone, the ink did not stick to the wetted surface but did stick to the applied image. Thus a print could be taken off the prepared stone. After many trials, which included the application of acid to the stone, Senefelder produced a printing process which was much cheaper than engraving and intaglio, and indeed produced a more pleasing and faithful reproduction of the original when applied to the colour separation techniques. Thus the marriage of lithography and colour separation began the commercial printing which dominates today.

The early lithographic artists used a fine line drawing on the stone to enable them to draw on it, in register, each printing colour, using not just the four that I have already mentioned but usually others too, especially pink and flesh tones to improve the artistic quality. Printing in ten colours was not rare even for commercial use, and it is possible with a magnifying glass to detect those extra colours in old specimens of printed work.

Photography began to be developed in 1827 and such men as Louis J. M. Daguerre and William Henry Fox-Talbot played a large part. It took a long time for the process to reach the commercial stage, with George Eastman introducing the roll-film camera in 1888. James Clerk Maxwell was the first to use colour filters to separate a colour subject into component colours, and then the invention of the half tone screen enabled the use of tiny dots to begin the replacement of chromolithography. The dots in a piece of modern printing may be easily observed with a magnifying glass; they are of different sizes thus giving the variation of colour required. The dots are generated by a half tone screen within the camera unit so that the photographic plate is divided up into many small dots. For lower quality printing such as for newspapers, it is usual to have 133 dots per inch. At Waddingtons, for playing cards we used 175 dots per inch and prided ourselves on it. In about 1960, we learned from Bob Lewin's company, Brett Litho of New York, how to print 300 dots per inch and from then on we used that process for postage stamps.

With the arrival of all these inventions and developments, the stage was set for tremendous growth in printing; Leeds was one centre which grew rapidly. Records show that in 1851, there were forty-one printing companies in Leeds which employed 800 people. By 1900 there were 170 companies with 7000 employees. Letterpress was the predominant printing process, but lithography was growing more quickly. Chromolithography clung on for a long time. When I started at Waddingtons in 1953, we were still producing posters with a large room full of skilled artists drawing directly onto aluminium or zinc plates. Metal plates had replaced the stones. Each plate was given a grained finish by being placed in a large vibrating tray, with emery powder and water worked onto the plate by glass marbles. The grained finish acted in the same way as the surface of the limestone, holding a thin film of water while the printing image repelled the water and accepted the ink. I introduced photolithography in our poster department with a massive camera capable of taking photographic plates of sixty inches by forty inches. The lithographic artists could still produce a better effect but only by using more than four colours. This made the process expensive and it was soon replaced. It was sad for the highly skilled artists, and I wonder if this art is still employed anywhere in the world.

In addition to the development of lithography, colour separation and photography, came the new machines. The rotary press was devised. Instead of a heavy flat stone, zinc or aluminium plates were wrapped around a printing cylinder so speeds increased from 800 per hour to 4000 per hour, and soon there were two-colour machines. Nowadays, reel fed presses print four colours on each side of the paper at 40,000 impressions per hour, and the skill of the operator is employed in managing the electronics and robotics of the machines.

All the recent developments in printing have been great for society but bad news for printers. Supply exceeds demand all the time. But in my grandfather's day the market was being created by the industry and demand was high. Victor Watson eagerly grasped the opportunities presented by developments which he understood. While others stayed still, he moved Waddingtons forward.

CHAPTER SEVEN

ENTER THE GAME MONOPOLY

IN ACQUIRING THE rights to the game of Monopoly, Victor Watson acted with entrepreneurial brilliance in a move which set the company on the road to greatness in the toy trade of the UK. It cannot be overemphasized that playing cards and games played a very important part in the progress of Waddingtons. In the second half of the twentieth century, games accounted for between ten and fifteen per cent of the company's sales, with packaging being the largest part, but games made the company famous and it is probably true that in the 1930s the presses were kept rolling by the printing of miniature and full size playing cards for the gift scheme of the Wills Tobacco Company. In the early days, Waddingtons had a few playing card games such as 'Shop Missus', 'Bob's Yr Uncle', 'Strip Tease' (great publicity), and 'Lexicon', which was the most successful of all. It was Lexicon which created the opportunity for Waddingtons to get Monopoly, because it gave the company credibility.

The acquisition by Waddingtons of the licence to publish Monopoly in the UK has already been related by Doug Brearley:

> On a certain Friday night towards the end of 1935, Victor Watson handed his son, Norman, a game with the remark, 'Look this over and tell me what you think about it'. It is recorded that Norman Watson said: 'I played an imaginary game against myself continuing through Friday night, Saturday night and Sunday night. I was enthralled and captivated. I had never found a game so absorbing, and thus Monopoly was first played in England at my home. I was so enthusiastic that on the Monday morning I persuaded my father to make a telephone call to Parker Brothers of Salem, Massachusetts, USA, the holder of the rights. Today transatlantic telephone calls are

commonplace, but this was the first one ever made by Waddingtons and I was told it was the first one ever received by Parker Brothers from Europe, so that, apart from its far-reaching consequences, the call itself was something of a landmark.' A licence arrangement was agreed on the phone and an exchange of letters followed.

That exchange was the only written agreement until well after the 1939–46 war.

The origin of the game Monopoly is well-documented in a book by Phil Orbanes called *Monopoly®: The World's Most Famous Game and How it Got That Way*. The popular story is that Monopoly was invented by an unemployed heating engineer called Charles Darrow of Philadelphia. He is said to have designed it on a piece of oilcloth on his kitchen table in about 1933 and sold copies to a few friends for four dollars each. However, Monopoly did in fact have a predecessor, which was entitled 'The Landlord's Game', and was invented by Elizabeth Magie in the USA in 1904. Miss Magie designed the game to illustrate the Single Tax theory, which proposed that the only thing to be taxed should be land or real estate. In 1924 she married Albert Phillips, revised her game and offered it, a second time, to Parker Brothers of Salem. George Parker, the President and owner of the company, turned it down once again as it was not much fun to play and took too long to complete a game.

Mrs Phillips' revised game of 1924 included a new feature – a monopoly rule by which a player owning all the railroads or utilities could charge a higher rent. She also added chips which could be used to improve the properties and increase the rents.

The game was played from 1904 onwards in some colleges in Eastern Pennsylvania and probably elsewhere in the USA, and changes were made. At one or more of those establishments arose the improvements which transformed The Landlord's Game into Monopoly. The outstanding feature of Monopoly is that a player may acquire the sets of the same colour and then build houses to increase the rent. Without this feature the game is lifeless. With it, Monopoly became, and remains, the greatest board game that has ever been known. Nobody knows who conceived that outstanding feature.

By the mid 1920s, the game with this new feature included became known as 'Monopoly'. Charles Darrow came across the game in 1933. A woman named Ruth Hoskins moved from Indiana to Atlantic City, bringing with her a copy of a game called 'Finance', made by Knapp Electric and 'invented' by Dan Layman. It had most of the features that we know in Monopoly, except that properties had to be auctioned when landed upon. Dan Layman had played The Landlord's Game in college, knocked Finance together, and sold it to a publisher.

Ruth Hoskins made a new game board based on Atlantic City and played it with her friends, who in turn played the game with a friend of Charles Darrow. When Darrow saw it he fell in love with it and made his own set, but kept the Atlantic City names. A previous inventor had mis-spelt the yellow property called, on the board, Marvin Gardens (in reality it is Marven Gardens), and Darrow innocently continued with that name, giving a vital clue to later investigations into the origin of the game Monopoly.

Incidentally, Atlantic City is one of the few cities in the USA to have names rather than numbers for its streets. This made for a much more interesting Monopoly board, although it was not half as good as the London board with names like Mayfair, Piccadilly and The Old Kent Road.

Charles Darrow styled the game board as we know it today and took his version of Monopoly to Parker Brothers, who rejected it in 1934. So, he began to make and sell it himself. It was a success. Parker Brothers' new President, Robert Barton (son-in-law of George Parker, the founder), met Darrow and arranged to publish the game. Shortly afterwards, Parker Brothers bought the patent of The Landlord's Game from Mrs Magie Phillips. They also bought the rights to the game Finance and two other similar games. Later on a licence was granted to Milton Bradley to publish the rival game 'Easy Money', which looked different to Monopoly but had the same playing features.

The story of the origin of Monopoly was never revealed to us at Waddingtons and I believe that the reason was that Robert Barton, the President of Parker Brothers, knew all along that Charles Darrow had not invented it. However, it made good sense to have a strong patent and copyright with Darrow as the inventor, and that is why Bob Barton acquired ownership of rival games such as Finance. The truth began to emerge in the 1970s when Ralph Anspach published 'Anti-Monopoly', a game which was supposed to expose the low ethics of business. Parker Brothers tried to stop Anti-Monopoly, but in his defence Anspach revealed such things as the mis-spelling of Marvin Gardens, one of the properties on the Monopoly board; he claimed such discrepancies proved the earlier development of Monopoly, rather than its invention by Darrow. In the end General Mills (the company which was by then the owner of Parker Brothers) made a deal with Anspach, and both games continued with Anti-Monopoly not doing very well.

The involvement of Waddingtons has been correctly chronicled by Douglas Brearley and Phil Orbanes. My grandfather, Victor Watson, spoke to Robert

Barton on the phone and convinced him that Waddingtons was the company to publish Monopoly under licence. Waddingtons was a very successful playing card maker by that time, but the company had only a few card games to its credit, including Lexicon, so it was an ambitious and entrepreneurial decision to take up this new game – easy to approve with hindsight.

As Doug Brearley showed in his article, Monopoly rapidly found a fan base at Waddingtons:

> When thinking and deciding how to change this American game into a British game by altering the names of the Atlantic City streets to London streets, a number of Waddingtons executives became so engrossed that they were playing the game instead of working. Wherever Monopoly was played, the players found they could not leave it alone and it became an addiction. The names of the streets and railway stations were the only alterations made. Like the rules of chess, the rules were left unchanged; and although property values are so different today, when Waddingtons have been asked to alter Monopoly values, the answer has always been 'no'.

The story of the choosing of the Monopoly sites based on London is largely true. Victor Watson and his secretary Marjorie Phillips did it together, and at the end of a morning taxi ride had tea at the Angel Islington, which by then was a Lyons tea shop, having previously been a pub. (It is now a branch of the Co-operative Bank.) Rather than look further, the Angel Islington was chosen for the last site on the Monopoly board and it has been the odd one out ever since. Monopoly was a success from the start, and it put Waddingtons on the map in the toy trade. Games inventors thought of the company and such great games as Waddingtons 'Buccaneer' followed.

The relationship between Parker Brothers and Waddingtons suffered during the war, which is why my father, Norman Watson, went to the USA in 1946 on a small cargo/passenger ship. He established a rapport with Bob Barton who met him in New York and said, 'Norman. I'll not agree to a continuation of the licence unless you come to stay with me at my home, 15 Chestnut Street in Salem, Massachusetts. I don't want you to go back to England with the idea that New York is the USA.' So Dad stayed with Bob and Sally Barton, enjoyed the log fires in their charming old house and met many good and friendly people. He did come back with a new and better view of that wonderful nation, and the business letters between Bob and Norman often included paragraphs on political matters which they enjoyed.

Waddingtons had many successes to follow Monopoly, but none to touch 'Cluedo', which was published in 1948. It became a great success in the USA as well. In the game, the Reverend Green became Mr Green, as Bob Barton of Parker Brothers thought that the American public would object to a parson being a murder suspect. They also changed the name to 'Clue'. Sales were huge and have continued to be so. For many years after that, Waddingtons made steady progress in the games field and profits were consistently good.

By 1968 my father was still the chairman of Waddingtons but delegated the work to me as the managing director, as he was unwell for much of the time. However he did rally when we received a great shock in February 1968. Out of the blue we learned that Parker Brothers had sold out to General Mills, a large company based in Minneapolis and famous for wheat products such as 'Cheerios', the breakfast cereal. However, even their famous 'Betty Crocker' cakes failed to arouse enthusiasm among the financiers. So General Mills decided to become a conglomerate, reckoning that their marketing skills in the grocery field could be applied to toys, games, jewellery, clothing and goodness knows what else. In 1965 they had enlisted Craig Nalen, the son-in-law of one of their senior executives Sewell Andrews, to head their toys and games empire, which was to be built by acquisition. Parker Brothers was his third acquisition and easily the most expensive. The price was about eighteen times net earnings, a very large multiple by the standards of those days. The margins enjoyed by Parker Brothers were very high, and to make the acquisition pay off Craig Nalen faced the task of improving them. A book called *Playing by Different Rules* by Eileen Wojahn chronicles the General Mills/Parker Brothers takeover, but my interpretation differs from hers. She seemed to assume that Waddingtons retained the Monopoly licence because of an old boy network or sentiment. In truth it was the strength of the game Cluedo in the USA which proved to be decisive. In her book, Miss Wojahn also says that Eddie Parker and his cousin Ranny Barton persuaded Ranny's father Bob, the President of Parker Brothers, that the company should seek a partner such as General Mills. I remember Bob Barton's explanation of the deal. He was concerned, he said, that the family had all its eggs in one basket, that board games seemed to be under pressure from other entertainment, that a sell-out seemed to make sense. He also said how much he admired General Mills and how well and courteously he had been treated by them. And the price was high. General Mills paid $45,500,000 for Parker Brothers.

At Waddingtons, what upset us was that Parker Brothers left us in the lurch. They could have arranged longer term contracts for Monopoly and

Cluedo. We were faced with the stark fact that the Monopoly licence could be cancelled with just one year's notice. What I learned later was that General Mills had insisted on secrecy, and only a limited number of people were let into that secret. Also, Ranny Barton and Ed Parker were convinced that Clue would be such a powerful weapon that Waddingtons would be able to keep the Monopoly licence.

Craig Nalen's idea from the start was to beef up the marketing and selling of his toy and game division. He wanted to do what the likes of Kodak, Coca Cola and Colgate had done around the world. His dream was that Monopoly would be an international brand, with an identical appearance and similar marketing programmes everywhere. He had no interest in pandering to the different preferences of the markets of the world. And so the negotiations began to relieve Waddingtons of the Monopoly licence; the persuasion, the veiled threats, the temptations. But Waddingtons had a trump card – the game Cluedo. Its sales in the USA far outshone the UK sales of Monopoly. I let it be known that we would contemplate taking the Clue licence from Parker Brothers and giving it to one of their rivals. I even established contact with Parker Brothers' hated enemy, Milton Bradley, met their people, and made no secret of it. News travelled fast in the toy trade in those days. In dealing with Craig Nalen, I was helped by his boss, Don Swanson and by General Mills' legal counsel Cliff Whitehill. Cliff pointed out that the Monopoly trademark was stronger in the UK than anywhere in the world. (This was at the time that Ralph Anspach had introduced Anti-Monopoly and the court proceedings were beginning.) Don Swanson obviously cautioned a more moderate approach to international affairs. So, in a year or so, we agreed to continue with licensing and a longer term agreement was signed.

I got on well with Craig Nalen and his wife and we had some good times together, but he fell out of favour for some reason or other and was replaced by the brilliant Bernie Loomis, who was not troubled by doubts about his own ability. Nalen had stolen Loomis from Mattel to run Kenner, General Mills' Cincinnati-based toy company. Loomis was famous for introducing such products as 'Hot Wheels'. At Kenner I believe he was also responsible for the introduction of Star Wars products, having got to know the film producer Stephen Spielberg well. They had dozens of Star Wars products in the Kenner range and even in other General Mills companies, and they were a huge success. Yes, Bernie Loomis was a great product and marketing man. However, his appointment as chief executive of General Mills' toy division did not suit everybody in the business, especially those in the international section. He stirred the pot. He seemed to believe that all the international subsidiaries, whether run by nationals or by Americans, were hopeless in their inability or unwillingness to operate as one great unified marketing machine. He had some executives who adopted a confrontational stance so far as Waddingtons were concerned. I remember very vividly the evening when a few of us were having dinner with their executive Jeff Jacobsen in London. We were trying to develop a better relationship. Eventually, I said that it would be good for both companies if they should licence Waddingtons with products like the best-selling card game, 'Pit', which we had had in the old days. I said, 'It seems, Jeff, that you are withholding products from us to make us weak so that you may pick up Waddingtons when we are in financial trouble.' He said 'Yes, that's right', and we were all stunned by his candour and by his naivety. I wrote a long letter to him on the subject, suggesting that a friendly co-operation would be beneficial to both companies. Shortly afterwards I got a phone call from Jim Boosales, an old Parker executive, who told me that he had just rejoined the group to be in charge of the international division, and that Jeff Jacobsen had been removed. He said, 'I am wading through Jeff's in tray and I have just come to your letter. I agree with every word of it and from now on we will be more like partners.'

The occasionally strained relationship with Kenner Parker did not stop the World Monopoly Championships. In fact, considering the worldwide popularity of the game, national and international Monopoly competitions came rather late. The first truly international competition was held in 1975 in Washington DC. Prior to this we in the UK organised a European Championship. The idea to stage what was ultimately a great publicity stunt developed from the success of smaller events, like the Tycoons' Monopoly game in 1970. The official account omits the background to this game. It was organised in conjunction with David Malbert, the well-known and highly rated finance editor of the *London Evening News*. He played in the game and acted as commentator for the TV audience. The game was played in the afternoon and excerpts were shown on the evening TV news, with a great many visits to the action and a final longer piece right at the end where the winner was crowned. Four of the players were well known for their entrepreneurial success and their wealth. Jim Slater had built up a conglomerate called Slater Walker by using shares to buy companies, and then with share price increases he would buy even more companies. Oliver Jessell had built up a secondary bank. However, the thriving businesses of Jim Slater and Oliver Jessell did not survive the financial turmoil that came later. Nigel Broackes had a property empire and the Cunard shipping line, and he stayed the course to become a permanent success. Jack Cohen had formed the supermarket chain Tesco, the 'co' of Tesco being from Cohen and the 'Tes' from the name of his wife. We also had Robert Morley, a well-known actor and wit. He was there like a court jester. We all had lunch beforehand while they set up the cameras next door. At the lunch Robert Morley started to laud the glory of the Soviet system. He may have done it to aggravate the capitalists at the table but he spoke as if he meant it, and told us how successful the Russians were and how the people were happier. Nobody believed him but we all listened and did not take the bait. But in the end Jack Cohen took Robert to task. 'I know about it,' he said, 'I come from Lithuania. I have relations there. It is bad – very bad.' He then proceeded to tell us of the terrors of the Soviet system and the inefficiencies, the oppression and the lack of freedom, and he forecast the inevitable end to it all. He quelled Morley very decisively. He also made me warm to him, so that I helped him to play his game of Monopoly. The contestants came with varied approaches. Broackes and Jessel treated it as a bit of fun. Jim Slater had been training and was determined to win. Jack Cohen had been given a few tips by his chauffeur but had not played the game. But Jack had that ingredient which can make up for lack of experience. He landed on Mayfair and Park Lane. I was the referee, but I nevertheless told Jack Cohen that if he wished, he could mortgage everything else and put houses on the expensive property. Jim Slater was furious. 'The referee shouldn't help the players,' he said. I replied that I was merely telling Jack the rules; it was untrue of course and they all laughed. Jack went on to win and had a great photo of himself in the papers with cigar in one hand, Monopoly money in the other. The publicity was extensive. The Tycoons' Monopoly game was a great success.

In 1975 we had the idea of a European Championship, preceded by National Championships and followed by a World Championship in Washington DC. It was planned for the autumn (fall) for maximum publicity leading up to Christmas. Parker Brothers agreed wholeheartedly.

Not long before this event the US chess master, Bobby Fischer, had challenged the Russian champion Boris Spassky to a world championship match and Reykjavik, the capital of Iceland, was chosen as the venue. Fischer produced new moves, which were a revelation to the world of chess. He and his team took Spassky's team by surprise by departing from tried and tested openings and early game development. Fischer won and achieved world fame; for some reason the match had captured the imagination of many. All of this gave us the idea of a Monopoly Championship in Iceland. It took place when the tourist season was over, so we got a very good price from

Icelandic Airways at their own hotel which was called the Loftleidr. Over ten European countries participated and most of them came to London to join the flight to Reykjavik. So on a cool autumn morning we set off with champions, company representatives, PR people and lots of press and TV crews. The championship lasted for three days with occasional time off for sightseeing and fun. The first highlight was the informal press championship the night before the real final. We started at eleven o'clock at night, and after an evening of carousing the players were in great form. Cheating was allowed, and along with much badinage, diversions, appeals to the referee, in fact all but actual fighting, it was a hilarious evening.

The second highlight was the final next day. One outsider was the Irish champion, John Mair. He had been at the press event while the other finalists were in bed early in order to be ready for the fray. John arrived for the final a bit late, obviously the worse for wear and carrying a gin and tonic. He caused a gale of laughter when he accidentally on purpose put the dice into his gin and tonic. John's money and properties were in a mess in front of him. He really did seem to be in a dream. When the big trading session began he was quiet but then he volunteered an idea and an offer just gently. Then he began to play a greater part. When all the trading was done and the players laid out the sets that each had acquired, we saw that John had gained a great position. He went on to win the game. He proved yet again that one should not be too assertive at Monopoly, but gain the confidence, respect and even friendship of the other players. No championship has been won by an objectionable person. Almost all the winners have been able to get on with people. Monopoly is like life in that respect as well as in the technical trading and money management.

From Iceland we went on to Washington DC, where John Mair was the victor against stiff opposition, including all the other European players who came too. The whole exercise was expensive but the resulting worldwide publicity was well worth it. It also set a standard for future events which the press of many countries looked forward to. The reporters in the UK vied with each other to participate in what became very popular junkets with good stories and good pictures.

In the UK we tried to choose unusual places for the National Championships. Two interesting examples were the railway platform at Fenchurch Street Station, one of the Monopoly board sites, and a nuclear power station, where the final was on the reactor itself. The 1991 event at the Cafe Royal in Regent Street (a Monopoly site) was played with real money, which gave the press much to talk about.

The World Championships which I was involved in after 1975 were as follows:

1977	Monte Carlo at the Hotel de Paris
Winner:	Kwa Chong Seng of Singapore
1980	Bermuda at the Southampton Princess
Winner:	Cesare Bernabei of Italy
1983	Palm Beach at the Breakers Hotel
Winner:	Greg Jacobs of Australia
1985	New York and Atlantic City at Claridge Casino
Winner:	Jason Bunn of England (Now a Leeds taxi driver)
1988	London at the Park Lane Hotel
Winner:	Ikuo Hiyakuta of Japan
1992	Berlin at the Grand Hotel Esplanade
Winner:	Joost Van Orten of Holland
1996	Monte Carlo at Loew's Hotel
Winner:	Christopher Yuen of Hong Kong

All of these championships up to 1992 were organised with great input from Waddingtons. The 1996 event, after the sale of Waddingtons Games to Hasbro in 1994, was run by Hasbro. I was still invited though, and I ran the book on the result whilst wearing my usual boater with the Union Jack ribbon. The championships were all joyous events, keenly fought but with excellent sportsmanship and much fun after the games. They were costly but the publicity pay-off was good and sometimes exceptional. I will give just one example. At the start of the 1977 event in Monte Carlo, I was surveying the scene from just inside the door to the ballroom when a lady arrived and seemed to be looking around for help. I introduced myself and found that she was an invited press representative and had just come to town on the sleeper from Paris. So I saw that she was checked in and had a good room and waited for her to come down. Then it transpired that she worked for *Readers Digest*. The result of her stay and the good hospitality and information she received from us culminated in a long article with pictures which appeared in millions of copies of *Readers Digest* worldwide. Yes, the championships were worthwhile!

We also proved to a sometimes sceptical press that skill was of paramount importance. A number of players like Dana Termans of the USA, Greg Jacobs of Australia and Mike Grabsky of Britain more than once reached the finals by dint of skilful play. In my opinion, Greg Jacobs could have won the 1985 event in Atlantic City as the game was locked up with no player owning a set. But we would have had to wait for a long battle of attrition and it would have been boring. So Greg sportingly led the way with a few trades of properties which enabled Jason Bunn to win. I could go on. The stories are many, and they all originate from a board game which was of enormous importance to Waddingtons.

CHAPTER EIGHT

PLAYING CARDS AND DE LA RUE

'LARGE STREAMS FROM LITTLE FOUNTAINS FLOW. TALL OAKS FROM LITTLE ACORNS GROW' – DAVID EVERETT (1769–1818)

THE FRIENDSHIP BETWEEN two competitors, my grandfather, Victor Watson, and Bernard Westall, the managing director of Thomas De La Rue Ltd, was the acorn from which something of great significance developed. In this account I tell of what followed in later years.

My grandfather, having got Waddingtons onto an even keel, started to look around for a speciality. He had noticed that printers who had developed their own products or markets performed better than the rest. He had two especial loves, music and playing cards, and his thoughts moved in those directions. There were only two makers of playing cards in Britain, Thomas De La Rue, London, and Goodall and Son, London, so my grandfather believed that there must be room for a third manufacturer. Imports were not a problem at the time because all playing cards had to be enveloped in duty wrappers, which had to be purchased from Customs and Excise. Waddingtons therefore started the extremely difficult task of learning how to make playing cards in 1920.

Progress was costly and slow, but was helped when Thomas De La Rue Ltd bought Goodalls in 1922. This made some of the Goodalls people unhappy and willing to join Waddingtons. The production process was fraught with difficulty. The cards had to be opaque, they had to slip through the fingers but not too much, they had to be uniform in size and the printing had to be exact so that all the cards had identical backs. My grandfather reckoned that the Waddingtons people were equal to the task and that success in playing cards would prove the excellence of the company's printing and also be a money spinner on its own. The difficulties were overcome and a reasonable incursion into the market was made. Then the idea of a radical new process came to mind. I do not know who first had the idea, but I would guess that it grew out of discussions with Harold Beasley and Gordon French. They were two very bright engineers who had left E. S. and A. Robinson in Bristol to set up their own company, Beasley French Ltd, which designed and manufactured machinery for envelope making. Grandfather and Dad were friendly with the two engineers, and no doubt they were impressed by the great speed of the envelope machines and wondered if playing cards could be produced by a reel-fed printing and punching process.

I remember, as a small boy, the early days of the process and its development. A factory was rented in Keighley. Why? Because it was off the beaten track. They wanted it to be away from the prying eyes of the printing trade and suppliers and their salesmen. After many experiments and trials, the final process had a reel of material with three cards side by side, punched holes to maintain good register, letterpress printing of the pips and the new process, gravure, for the face side. It was a sedate but elegant contraption, and eventually it worked really well. As a small boy I was fascinated by it. The ink had to dry before the varnishing and calendering process and so the reel ran up and down the four-storey building through holes in the floors. Although slow, the output per person was amazingly large by the standards of those days. And the gravure process for the backs gave great consistency of colour. This meant that the reject rate was low and the examination was quicker. It was a revolution in playing card manufacture and it put Waddingtons into a very strong position.

During the development of the new equipment, my grandfather received a communication from Mr Lamert, the chairman of De La Rue, inviting him to call to see something very interesting. My grandfather duly called, whereupon he was shown a letter which was anonymous and which offered to De La Rue the secrets of the new Waddingtons process. If he wanted to accept the offer, Mr Lamert had to place a notice in a particular newspaper. Instead, the honourable gentleman gave the letter to my grandfather. Back at the factory in Leeds, my father compared the typewriting with the lettering from all the suppliers and found that it matched those from Crabtrees, the electrical engineers in Shipley, near Bradford. My grandfather and father went to see Mr Crabtree who looked at the letter and said, 'It must be Bernard, one of the designers'. Bernard was sent for, confronted with the evidence and admitted that he was the culprit. (Although not essentially part of this account, it is interesting to note that Bernard was known to my grandfather as the son of a professor of Leeds University. Grandfather had reason to be sorry for Bernard, who was so unruly as a boy that he was often chained to a leg of the kitchen table.) He was admonished by Mr Crabtree and taken off the job, but not dismissed. How different from today, with all our pious regulatory bodies to ensure good behaviour! The gentlemanly attitude of Sidney Lamert in regard to this event was probably the beginning of years of fair and friendly rivalry between De La Rue and Waddingtons.

The dominance of De La Rue was challenged by the upstarts. So the managing director of De La Rue, Bernard Westall, decided to visit Leeds to confront the other two British playing card makers. (By that time, the early 1930s, Alf Cooke Ltd had also set up a playing card department.) Bernard Westall's first call was to Alf Cooke himself, who said that he would be willing to fix prices but that the fellow up the road, that brigand and buccaneer Victor Watson, would never agree to any such collusion. Bernard Westall called on Victor Watson as soon as he had left Alf Cooke. It was a taxi ride of just two miles. The two men were opposites. Victor Watson left school at the age of twelve; Bernard Westall went to Cambridge University. Victor Watson had been an apprenticed lithographer; Bernard Westall was the son of a Church of England Bishop and had been born with the proverbial silver spoon in his mouth. Victor Watson had a Yorkshire accent. Bernard Westall had an accent and indeed a way of speaking which made him completely at ease at Henley, Ascot or Lords. He was of a military appearance and demeanour; tall, moustached, alert and almost jumpy in manner. He was full of energy, life and laughter. Yes, they were poles apart socially, but they hit it off. They both loved playing bridge, chess, cricket, indeed all the games. They sparked off each other and enjoyed the rivalry and the comradeship which often develop alongside such interactions. After meetings in Leeds and London, they agreed that price fixing would eventually destroy the competitive edge of both businesses and make them vulnerable to attack from others. Instead, they instituted an annual cricket match and other events so that the executives of both businesses would get to know each other, and thus compete fairly and without resorting to anything like unsporting behaviour.

Then the war came. In 1941, De La Rue's factory in Bunhill Row, London, was destroyed in the Blitz. Victor Watson was in London at the time, staying at the Waldorf Hotel as he always did. He heard of the disaster and went at once to Bunhill Row, where he found Bernard Westall ruefully regarding the ruins and trying to get people together to salvage what they could. Victor said, 'We can't have the Jerries interfering with our rivalry. For as long as the war lasts, De La Rue can have half of Waddingtons' playing card production. We can keep the sales forces separate but manufacture jointly.' The Amalgamated Playing Card Company was formed and it proceeded to operate in Leeds and Keighley under a joint board, but it was actually run by my father and his assistant Doug Brearley. In addition, in 1941, Waddingtons undertook much of De La Rue's banknote printing work and rented out part of its Leeds factory to De La Rue. This arrangement lasted until 1962, when De La Rue realised that they had to build and equip a specialised factory to keep pace with the many changes of technology in the security printing business at that time.

The association of De La Rue and Waddingtons was of great benefit to both companies. It was more than a mere business relationship. It was based on friendship. Bernard Westall was a leader, a man of vision; one who people enjoyed working for because he was imaginative and decisive. He was a man of humanity, capable of great friendship. And he loved life. In the later years when the commercial arrangement between De La Rue and Waddingtons had ended, Bernard Westall continued to be a director of Waddingtons' monthly journal, *Bridge Magazine*. He used to come to Leeds once a year for the annual general meeting with my father, my Uncle Horace, Clac Prudhoe (the De La Rue executive who stayed with Waddingtons to run the playing card business) and me as the lad. I wrote the minutes. For example: 'Champagne was served and the directors congratulated each other on the small loss which had been incurred during the year under review.' After the mid-morning meeting we went to Moortown Golf Club for lunch, played golf in the afternoon, then snooker, then dinner and then bridge. When Bernard was about eighty years old, I remember him saying to me, 'I wake up in the morning, say "I've got another day!" and then I pack as much into the day as I can.' I have always remembered that positive attitude, just as I will always remember a remarkable man.

Eventually, De La Rue tired of the playing card business and sold out to Waddingtons. By that time Waddingtons' sales of No.1 Playing Cards had far outstripped the sales of De La Rue's brand called Crown. It happened in this way. For many, many years every pack of playing cards in Britain had to be wrapped in a customs and excise duty wrapper, which cost three pence (in the days when it was 240 pence to the pound). The wrappers had to be purchased from HM Customs and Excise and applied by hand. It was a crazy, anachronistic system, but it was an effective barrier to imports, so nobody complained until a bright lad called Martin Foley came on the scene. De La Rue sometimes put their new recruits into their stationery division for experience. Martin Foley was such a one and he found himself in charge of the sales of playing cards. He made representations to HM Treasury to have the duty wrapper abolished, and in the Budget of 1960 it was announced that the change was to be made. My father was beside himself with rage at the folly of Foley, but when he calmed down he had a brainwave. The duty wrapper had always seemed to be like a guarantee of quality and security, so Dad decided to apply Waddingtons' own seal which looked like the old duty wrapper; it is still used to this day, and I have advised Hasbro to retain it for its effectiveness. De La Rue just put Crown playing cards in a plain box with no seal or wrapper. The sales of Waddingtons No.1 Playing Cards and Crown had been neck and neck. Within months of the change in appearance, the sales of No.1 went up and the sales of Crown went down. The result was devastating for De La Rue. Although they owned half of the production company their sales were tiny. They decided to abandon playing cards altogether and in 1967 sold their half of the Amalgamated Playing Card Company to Waddingtons. A side effect was that De La Rue lost the Royal Warrant for supplying the Queen. That went to myself as managing director of Waddingtons, and eventually led to me getting myself on the Council of the Royal Warrant Holders Association and becoming President in 1983.

Waddingtons No.1 Playing Cards are still the best-sellers in Britain, but they are marketed by a company called Winning Moves, who bought the brand from Hasbro, together with Lexicon. (Hasbro bought Waddingtons Games Ltd in 1994.) The cards are now imported. There is now just one maker of playing cards in Britain, Richard Edward of London.

CHAPTER NINE

ANOTHER ACORN, ANOTHER TALL OAK

FROM SATONA TO PLASTIC CONTAINERS

The story of the early days of the Satona packaging system is told in Doug Brearley's article on the history of Waddingtons. The development of this side of the business after the 1930s had most unexpected ramifications. For a start, there was a dreadful blow at the end of the war, because the raw materials needed to manufacture cartons had increased in price by ten times, so the package could not compete against the old glass bottle. In addition to this, almost all the milk in Britain was delivered to the doorstep. In contrast, in the USA, milk was largely sold by shops, so there was a more likely market for the non-returnable package made of paperboard. The Ex-Cell-O Corporation in Detroit began to grow a very large business with the Pure-Pak system, with filling plants installed in dairies and folding carton manufacturers licensed to produce the blanks (later on the reels of board).

But Satona was not dead. The company had a new chemist, Norman Gaunt, a man of formidable inventiveness and great energy. He developed a special wax for the Satona carton so that it would contain orange squash. This was a boon for the cinemas at a time when confectionery rationing still continued. J. Arthur Rank, on one occasion, announced to his shareholders that Rank Cinemas made more from the sale of orange squash than they did from the sale of the cinema seats themselves. Waddingtons' main customer was Schweppes. There were other suppliers and other cinema chains, but Schweppes and Rank were the largest. Waddingtons made a lot of money from Satona at that time.

As previously stated, the packaging of milk in paper in the UK was only small, whereas in the USA it was a huge business which was dominated by the Ex-Cell-O Corporation with their Pure-Pak packaging system. A huge investment was needed to make any impact on the market, so in the early 1960s Waddingtons got together with the International Paper Company of the USA and Metal Box, the powerful UK packaging company, and formed a tripartite company called Liquid Packaging. This enabled them to take an Ex-Cell-O licence, use the engineering capability of Metal Box and the market power of International Paper, and take on the newer competitors in the field of milk packaging. (This was before Tetra Pak, the packaging system that made the Rausing family one of the richest in the world.) Unfortunately, the united effort of the three companies was not sufficiently united, the competition was greater than expected and it was probably too early for the market anyway, so the new company did not last long.

As for the orange squash business, we at Waddingtons had already seen the writing on the wall. Rationing had ended, ice cream and sweets were available in the cinemas and Schweppes had faced the fact that Kia-Ora orange squash in a waxed carton was a poor product. The wax leached all the flavour out of the drink, it was only palatable when really cold and even then you couldn't detect the taste anyway. We were told to improve the package or come up with something new. This was the sort of challenge relished by Norman Gaunt and his able assistant Peter Harrison. They had already developed plastic coatings for use with frozen food cartons which had given Waddingtons a lead over the competitors, so the plastic coating was the first option to be tried. But Norman's inventive mind reasoned that the carton was a mere vehicle for the plastic, so why not do away with the carton and keep the plastic inside it? In other words, produce a thin wall plastic container for liquids. A new package called Plastona was developed with the help of Axel Homberg, the Danish engineer who had built the original Satona machines. The new system of thermoforming was used; this method was an advance on vacuum forming and used heat to soften the polystyrene and then employed both vacuum and air pressure to form the container. The innovation became a huge success. It was a 'tall tree' from the 'acorn' of Satona. Plastona Ltd became a large supplier of thermoformed containers made of polystyrene, polypropylene, ABS and other plastics. The customers ranged from Van Den Bergh's and Schweppes to many non-food companies such as Procter and Gamble.

CHAPTER TEN

THE BID OF 1967

IN MAY OF 1967, Mardon International of Bristol made an unwelcome bid for Waddingtons. The company had become an attractive target and there were already rumours of takeover bids. The quality of the company had grown through invention and development. My father, Norman Watson, believed wholeheartedly in inventors and was one himself in fact; it was through his reel-fed playing card process that the company was probably saved in the years of the 1930s Depression. Inventors need to be cherished and appreciated. I used to say, 'Invention is a fragile flower which may be crushed with a single harsh word.'

At Waddingtons, not only did we have a games development department by this stage, but also a small folding carton development section, which was instrumental in taking Harry Bradley's neat lamp bulb package and provoking a multitude of cartons for Easter eggs, which gave Waddingtons the lion's share of that business for years. Norman Gaunt, our talented chemist, developed plastic coatings for folding cartons which put us in the forefront of frozen food packaging. Norman and I were charged with adding a scientific dimension to our folding cartons and labels operation. We started to measure the humidity of the atmosphere in which we worked, the moisture content of the materials we used, the viscosity of the inks; indeed everything which had previously been part of the craft became the subject of measurement, analysis and hence understanding. Our greatest success was to get everybody interested and involved in the process. Waddingtons became leaders in folding cartons and paper labels. We supplied the best and most famous companies like Cadbury's, Rowntrees and Birds Eye, and we were the largest label supplier to H. J. Heinz. We had a quality control system which eventually became widely used in the industry. In the early post-war years Waddingtons also earned money from the supply of printing to De La Rue for bank notes, and made a fortune through the waxed Satona carton for Schweppes Kia-Ora orange drinks. Despite all these advances though, we were still old-fashioned printers with the contract to print 100,000 *Meccano Magazines* each month, and we still produced theatre programmes, a business which dated back to the company's beginning.

Our executives were encouraged to get out and about, to travel, to meet people in the trade, to find out what the customer wanted, to try to foresee what the customer would want if it was available; in fact, to understand the market place. In those post-war years when shortages and rationing were the main problem for British companies, a visit to the USA was an eye-opener. Bountiful produce, new ideas, prosperity; the opportunities to take up new ideas, products and processes were abundant. One such opening was created by greetings cards, with the new merchandising system called Retail Stock Control. Soon after the war, Waddingtons printed some greetings cards for a Canadian company called RustCraft. My father wrote a letter and had a copy of it put into each bale of print, addressed to whoever opened the bale. It was a letter of thanks to the Canadian people for their support during the war. A copy reached the managing director, Fred Cranston, and he approached my father with an invitation to participate in a British subsidiary of RustCraft. So Waddingtons bought the Leeds printing firm Cardigan Press (where my grandfather had worked at the turn of the nineteenth century), the name was changed to RustCraft, and the company became owned jointly by Waddingtons and RustCraft Canada. RustCraft USA was owned by United Printers, a group of greetings card and calendar companies which was run by a company doctor called Grant Gillam, who was from Chicago (he'd been put in charge by the banks). But RustCraft Canada was a separately owned business with Grant Gillam as a shareholder, which put him in a precarious position when United Printers was acquired by Raymond Lewenthal and Lew Birkman of Boston. They were not friendly towards Fred Cranston or his son Don (who worked for Waddingtons for a while), and they wanted to be rid of Waddingtons. After some stormy sessions of negotiation, Waddingtons sold its half of RustCraft. We then considered becoming the licensee of Norcross of New York and finally agreed a takeover of Valentines of Dundee with a licence from Norcross. Waddingtons now had a strong position in the field of greetings cards and giftwrap, and could take full advantage of the new merchandising system.

At this time we concluded a deal with Eureka in Scranton, Pennsylvania to produce trading stamps, mostly for Green Shield but also for the US giant, Sperry and Hutchinson. We had also entered the field of continuous stationery and business forms with three executives, Tony Mason, Jim Martin and Geoff Tapperell. We hired them from W. H. Smith who, at that time, had a large printery for stationery of all kinds.

So, by the time we caught the attention of Mardon International, Waddingtons' assets were extensive. We had a packaging division of quality, which included the new thermoforming of plastic containers. The publishing division boasted Waddington Games and Valentines of Dundee, along with a French playing card company which we shared with De La Rue. Printing included business forms, posters and advertising print, an Irish subsidiary, the Ormond Printing Company, and a new acquisition, Eagle Transfers, with a licence from the Meyercord Decalcomania Company of Chicago. Mardon's board obviously salivated at the thought of all this invention and development on a plate for their greater financial resources to be applied to and the whole world to go at. Mardon International was a four-year-old combination of Mardon, Son and Hall, which was the carton producing business of Imperial Tobacco, and the carton companies (world wide) of British American Tobacco. Mardon was four times the size of Waddingtons and truly international. It made good sense for them to acquire Waddingtons, especially for the plastic packaging unit and also for an entry into games and greetings cards.

The bid battle of 1967 began with a letter from Mardon's chairman, Desmond Misselbrook, to my father and at the same time a letter from Mardon's managing director, Hugh Carter (who I knew well), to me. They were polite and persuasive letters suggesting that we meet to discuss the proposed takeover. After much thought and advice from professional advisers we did meet. My father was ill and semi-retired at the time, so the work devolved on me and our vice-chairman, Everard Chadwick. We met Mardon three times in all and thought we had convinced them that they should go away. They did not go away, and later Everard Chadwick said to me that in future we should not do the decent thing and have conversations, but simply tell unwanted suitors that they were unwelcome. His very words were, 'We'll just tell them to bugger off.'

At this time, our merchant bank was Kleinwort Benson, and the executive who handled our account was Charles Ball, a highly intelligent man and a determined advocate.

Mardon decided that they would bid. On 17 May 1967 the bid was announced, but without any prices mentioned as they requested a meeting with us first. Together with our various bankers, we did meet and the bid was announced: 33*s*. 6*d*. for each voting share, and 32*s*. for each non-voting share, valuing Waddingtons at £4.4 million. With our advisers we decided that if the offer reached 45*s*. for each voting share we would have difficulty in defending the position. I wanted to tell the world what a great company Waddingtons was and how well we were doing, and yet at the same time I wanted to tell Mardon how likely we were to lose the Monopoly licence and also the licence for Norcross greetings cards if Mardon took over. Kleinwort Benson were not very happy at this idea, but Charles Ball of Kleinworts was empowered by us to discuss the situation with Lazards, the other side's bank, and to say that if the bid was 50*s*. for each voting share then we would recommend it. As a result of his talks, we met the Mardon people on 7 June 1967 and, although it seems incredible looking back on it, I gave an account of the company, including the breakdown of the profit (which had not yet been released to the shareholders) and a forecast of profit for the year ending in March 1968. How things have changed in what one is allowed to do on this score! The result of the meeting was that Mardon increased their bid before it was ever posted to shareholders, and we were told that this had never been done before. They increased to 39*s*. for each voting share and 37*s*. 6*d*. for each non-voting share. We continued to reject with vigour and *The Daily Telegraph* reported, 'Mardon face a formidable partnership in Mr Victor Watson, Waddingtons' independent-minded managing director, and Mr Charles Ball, the hands-off expert at Kleinwort Benson.'

I can remember that it was a good summer and that it was the year my wife had a very serious operation. I also remember how traumatic the whole situation was as we worked to fight off the bid, and how our determination to do so grew as the weeks went by. When we first started our campaign, Charles Ball seemed to think that gaining a high price would be gaining a victory. By the time we finished we had convinced him that only continued independence could be counted as a victory. The extraordinary thing is that the board of directors, together with family and friends, controlled forty-nine per cent of the votes by virtue of our voting and non-voting share structure. So it would seem that we could just have said to them, 'Go away. We reject.' But it was at a time when non-voting shares were becoming very unfashionable and very unpopular and, if we had adopted a cavalier attitude, the City would have taken a very dim view of it. We were advised that, regardless of votes, we should take into consideration the interests of the shareholding body at large. It is interesting to record that Everard Chadwick, our vice-chairman and legal adviser (of Hepworth and Chadwick), said to me, 'We may reach a stage where we as directors have to advise the shareholders that the price is fair and even recommend that they accept the offer. However, the directors are entitled to say "…but in relation to our personal shareholdings we do not intend to accept."' Everard also said that he intended to refuse the offer. What would have happened in that case is difficult to imagine. But at the same time my father, who was ill, said to me 'Perhaps we should accept the offer. You are too hard-pressed by the business and you take it all so much to heart that I fear for your health. You would do well to be working for them. The company would be immensely strong. And the family's fortune would be secure.'

In spite of the other side eventually raising the bid to 45s., we still won easily as they gained very few acceptances. I wrote in my file that the lessons learned were that determination pays, that the personal approach matters a great deal, and that the attitude of people and their ideas on what can and cannot be defended changes considerably during the course of a bid. Believe it or not, we never visited one institutional shareholder during that successful fight!

CHAPTER ELEVEN

THE BIDS OF NORTON AND WRIGHT AND MAXWELL IN 1983

A PRELUDE TO CHAPTERS ELEVEN AND TWELVE

There would be no takeover bids without public companies and their shareholders, and it is worth saying a few words about public companies as a prelude to these chapters on takeover bids. It is said that the invention of the limited liability company played a significant part in the industrial development and the enormous rise in the standard of living in this and other countries. Before that, the economy was characterised by agriculture, cottage industries and merchants. As Alvin Toffler lucidly describes in his book *The Third Wave*, limited liability and the joining together of investors enabled the concentration of resources, which led to mechanisation, standardisation, specialisation and maximisation – all features of the so-called industrial revolution of which we are beneficiaries.

Another important historical factor should also be borne in mind. Towards the end of the nineteenth century, Gladstone introduced tax relief on life assurance and pension contributions. It was done to help the professional classes and small businessmen. It had an unexpected and astonishing result, as so often happens with artificial fiscal arrangements. Life assurance and pension contributions became such a tax-efficient method of saving that within 100 years, very large bodies known as 'institutions' had become established, which received the savings of manufacturing companies and their employees. The institutions then became shareholders in the very companies that had invested in the institutions. As a result, we have now reached the stage where the small private shareholder is almost insignificant.[1]

Waddingtons was owned mostly by those institutions. And some of them, like Waddingtons, were also on the performance treadmill. There are now regular league tables showing which institutions are the best performers. It is thus tempting for them to take a short-term view, and a takeover bid can yield a very juicy short-term profit.

I deplore the takeover bids by greedy and acquisitive predators, who care for making money and for nothing else. But they can be likened to the vultures and scavengers of the system, and, like nature itself, a dynamic system needs vultures and scavengers. The alternative is socialism. The inefficiency and tyranny of socialism seem to me to be worse than 'the unacceptable face of capitalism' as it was called by Mr Heath, or, as it can be more pungently described, the 'effluent society – the stinking rich'.

---

1   CAVEAT
In case anybody checks my reference to the former Prime Minister of Great Britain, William Ewart Gladstone, I must admit that I have tried to do so and failed. The former City editor of United Newspapers, John Heffernan (whose excellent monthly newsletter, *The Bulletin*, can be acquired by email – john.heffernan@virgin.net) could find no reference, but said that he liked the idea I put forward. He said it was yet another example of the law of unexpected consequences. Then I discovered that in 1874 Gladstone wanted to abolish income tax, which was threepence in the pound at the time. (*Encyclopaedia Britannica*!) At such a low rate no tax concession would make a difference to people's financial decisions. Nevertheless, my general theory seems to be right. It is just a pity that factual confirmation is absent.

THIS IS MY personal account of the bids for Waddingtons in 1983. It is the battle as I saw it. There were others involved of course and they will all have seen it slightly differently, but I hope that my account accords with their recollection in the main. I was the chairman of Waddingtons at the time and still executive. David Perry was the managing director. I had finally persuaded him to join us, a task made easier by the fact that Robert Maxwell took over the British Printing and Communication Group (BPCC) and David found himself working for an unreasonable man. At the outset of the bids, we agreed that my first priority would be the bid defence while David ran the business. Our finance director, Chris Bowes, and company secretary, Peter Stephens, were closely involved in the bid battle. Other board members included Ken Lunn who, in effect, was David Perry's right hand man; Norman Gaunt, our brilliant technical director and deep thinker, who was a great asset; and my younger brother, John, aged forty at the time and the Member of Parliament for Skipton, who headed some of Waddingtons' companies and played a part at top level too. Our non-executive director was Tony Brown, the managing director of Rose Forgrove Ltd, the makers of packaging machinery.

All the directors were involved in the bid defence and many senior executives too. We had many meetings to settle plans and forecasts. Customers and suppliers and associates were keenly interested and some had positive assistance to offer. And towards the end of the bid we used many senior people to visit or telephone the shareholders who had not received personal approaches until that time.

After the bid of 1967 and before the 1983 bids for Waddingtons, the Stock Exchange introduced many rules concerning bids and also formed a Takeover Panel to act as referee. This self-regulation was widely thought to be preferable to legislation. The sanction which the Stock Exchange has within its powers is the withdrawal of a public company's quotation. Frankly, people seem to get away with far too much in spite of this discipline, but I suspect that if we had legislation the disreputable types would just find new ways of being devious.

The takeover rules which were of the greatest importance during our bid of 1983 were as follows:

Rule 10 (1)   Offer document must be posted within 28 days of announcement.

Rule 21 (1)   Offeror must have over 50% before offer can become unconditional.

Rule 22 (1)   Offer must be open at least 21 days after posting.
If revised, it must be kept open for at least 14 days after posting the revision.
An acceptor can withdraw his acceptance after 21 days from the first closing date.
If an offer is revised, all original acceptors must receive the revised consideration.

Rule 22 (2)   No offer can become unconditional after 3.30pm on the 60th day after the initial posting, except if there is a competing offer.
No offer may be revised after the 46th day after the initial posting.

Rule 24   The offeror shall announce the result by 9.30am on the day after the offer is due to expire.

Rule 32 (1)   If the offeror (a) buys shares during the offer period, or (b) holding more than 15% of the shares, has bought shares during the 12 months period before the offer above the offer price, then he shall increase the offer to the highest price which he has paid.

Rule 34 (1)   Any person who acquires 30% or more of the voting shares must make an offer for all those voting shares.

Rule 35   An offeror may not (a) make another offer, or (b) buy shares which put his shareholding up to 30% or more for 12 months after the offer has been withdrawn or has lapsed.

Rule 41   An offeror may not buy shares for 7 days after the intention to make an offer is announced.

In addition there were pages about verification of figures, directors' responsibility, privileged information – all of which are familiar to most businessmen.

The bids for Waddingtons, which caused such headlines over the seventeen weeks from 17 May 1983 to 17 September, were not wholly unexpected. The company had been through a bad time. Firstly the company suffered the Videomaster disaster. Video games hit the market in the mid- seventies and were hugely successful. Sales of traditional board games were knocked for six. It seemed that Waddingtons must enter the new market, which we did with the purchase of Videomaster. But the technical problems were great and the development costs high, and so large orders needed to be placed to get the unit cost down; then the market collapsed in 1980. Secondly, Waddingtons suffered the effects of inflation with the debilitating Prices and Incomes Policy, which formed part of the Government's futile attempt to control prices and incomes and keep inflation in check. To reduce our resulting indebtedness we sold Valentines of Dundee to Hallmark Cards for £4.1 million. The thought was that the sale made strategic sense, but it was prompted by the need to raise cash. However, our bad time encouraged us to modernise and economise. There were three major influences on business at this time; the poor economy, technological changes, and the new (1979) Conservative Government's laws to curb the ever increasing power of the Trade Unions. The most significant of these was the pace of technological change. Even the most recalcitrant union member could see that new methods had to be embraced. David Perry joined us in the spring of 1981 and became managing director a year later. His contribution to the revitalising of the business was crucial. He saw the company through new eyes, was not bound by old loyalties, knew of no sacred cows, and had knowledge and great energy. We amalgamated our various games companies and towards the end of 1982 rationalised our folding cartons business, all of this with many redundancies and accompanied by savage reductions across the board, including administrative staff.

The cost of all the savings and reorganisation was large, but it was all written off so that we could look forward to a better performance from 1983 onwards. In the early part of 1983, business improved in the UK and we also began to benefit from the success of our business in Canada, which was run by my brother Beric after a few years of retirement. In addition to this, the company recovered from the pain of the cost reductions remarkably quickly. Usually after major surgery in a company, there is a period of unsettlement when all the people are demoralised. It takes time to recover. In our case, the company just seemed to shrug its shoulders and march on as strongly as ever. I attributed this to the fact that we had always cared for our people, striven to serve our customers, and tried to maintain development and investment in the latest technology.

Profitability began to improve. It was a good time for a greedy predator to pounce. We made such plans as we could in readiness for a takeover attempt. I heard someone say, 'What makes God laugh most of all is to see men making plans.' We made a list of companies which might launch an unwelcome bid for Waddingtons; Norton and Wright were not on that list.

Internal Memo
From: Mr Victor H Watson   Date: 25 January 1983

I have been thinking about companies which may try to take us over and I have also been thinking about those we might prefer if our corrective action fails. Firstly I produced a list and discussed it with Roy Dearden of Cazenoves in December. The list and comments are as follows:

Competitors	*BPC*
	DRG
	Metal Box
	Reeds
	Bowaters
	Mardon
	Smurfit
	Linpac
	Esselte

So far as BPC and Maxwell are concerned Roy says that they are always likely and if anybody else bids then they will almost certainly join in. Maxwell is backed by Natwest Bank.

He thinks that DRG, Reeds and Smurfit are very unlikely. He says that Metal Box, Bowaters and Mardon might from what he knows, and I feel that they possibly could be interested in mopping up UK competitors and would, of course, be interested in Plastocan.

Roy knows nothing about Linpac and nor do I except that Harold Rogan told me that they would always be interested in buying Plastona.

Esselte might be interested in consolidating their UK position.

Conglomerates   BPB
　　　　　　　　Lonrho
　　　　　　　　Ferguson
　　　　　　　　Cope Allman
　　　　　　　　Hanson
　　　　　　　　Tilling
　　　　　　　　Central and Sheerwood

Roy thinks that Ferguson would be too small and that Cope Allman and Central and Sheerwood do not have the fire power. He thought that Tilling and Hanson would be very unlikely.

Lonrho are unpredictable and might very well be interested.

We did not discuss BPB because I had not thought of them at the time. Their sales are £400 million per annum in plaster board and the like and they own Davidson Radcliffe the board makers, and Landor cartons.

Others   *Mills and Allen*
　　　　　Norcros
　　　　　Low and Bonar
　　　　　Fine Art
　　　　　Pentos
　　　　　Bunzl
　　　　　Metal Closures
　　　　　Unilever
　　　　　General Mills
　　　　　Continental Can
　　　　　International Paper

Roy thinks we would be outside the scope of Mills and Allen. He does not know about Norcros but I know that they wanted to buy Waddingtons some years ago. He thinks that Fine Art and Pentos do not have the muscle, and since then I have heard that Fine Art have difficulties.

He thinks that Bunzl would be interested but not as an unwelcome predator.

Metal Closures are a possibility but would not want anything to do with our games side.

I don't know about Unilever but they might be interested in securing certain supplies and preventing the productive facilities falling into unwelcome hands.

So far as the foreigners are concerned I would think it very unlikely that they would be interested even if the approach was by us.

John Watson has mentioned McCorquodale as a possible predator. Frankly I think they are well off in the security field and with foreign activities and would not welcome our problems.

We have concluded that we should not contemplate selling out. Our plan is to cut costs and go all out for sales and ultimate success. We believe that this makes sense for the shareholders as suggested by Chris Bowes as follows:-

In the event of an agreed takeover it seems unlikely that the share valuation would be greater than 140p.

However, if we attain the projected profits of £1.5 million in 1983–84 and £2.8 million in the following year the dividend possibilities are interesting. We shall be paying no tax other than ACT:

Ordinary Dividend	Gross Cost Pref.	Ordy.	Total	Share Value (10% yield)	P/E Ratio 1.5m.	2.8m.
5p	40	446	486	-	-	-
10p	40	892	932	142p	5.9	3.2
15p	40	1338	1378	215p	9.0	4,8
20p	40	1784	1824	285p	-	6.3

In respect of 1984–85 a 20p dividend would not be out of the question. This would put a value of 285p on the shares with a very modest P/E ratio of 6.3.

This is probably more attractive to shareholders, than 140p now. We should bear in mind that if the company does achieve the profit forecast it will mean that we are doing well in new areas of activity and on a rising profit trend.

Chris Bowes was our finance director and his prophetic words are exceptionally interesting.

I was in Scotland on the morning of the bid of 17 May 1983, the anniversary of the earlier bid in 1967. Richard Hanwell, the thrusting managing director of Norton and Wright, called at our office just before 9.30am to see me, or anybody in charge, and had difficulty in finding anyone. He wanted to tell us the news before we heard it from the Stock Exchange, because the bid was indeed on its way via Norton and Wright's merchant bank, Samuel Montagu.

At this early stage we made our worst mistake. Not many people even recognized that a mistake had been made. But I know that we should have immediately told the shareholders not to sell their shares, as the price offered was far too low. To put this in perspective, our share price had been 68p only eight weeks before and Norton and Wright were offering 133p cash or 144p on a valuation of their shares. By 4.00pm on the following day, the price on the Stock Exchange was 166p. In those first two days a very large number of Waddingtons shares changed hands and obviously the new owners were less likely to have any loyalty. It was a mistake not to be positive and not to tell the shareholders to hold on.

At the same time Norton and Wright, if they had succeeded in their bid, could also have made a terrible mistake. They knew hardly anything about Waddingtons. They certainly did not know that we were on the point of obtaining a very large contract for the manufacture of plastic containers – a contract which would raise the profit of our plastics business. They did not know that the customer in question made it abundantly clear that if Norton and Wright acquired Waddingtons, that contract would go to one of our competitors, together with some of the business we already enjoyed – a disaster for our plastics business. But this is the sort of risk you take when you launch an unwelcome bid, particularly if it is for a company dealing in industrial rather than consumer products.

During the first phase of our defence campaign, which took place at the time of the general election, we instituted a crash programme to finalize our results, print a beautiful annual report and release it to the shareholders and the press. Our figures showed a considerable improvement and we wanted to get all this in before the closing date of Norton and Wright's offer, which was 20 June. By this time we had even better news to announce, as our April and May figures were good, but our merchant banker and broker said, 'Hold your fire. They won't get many acceptances at the first offer. They'll then increase and we must save something to say. Save your aces.' I can well remember on 16 June when I returned from London how our finance director and managing director told me that they had heard from another source that Norton and Wright had been visiting our shareholders and gathering support. They said, 'It's all very well saving the aces, but suppose the game is over and we still have the aces in our hand?' Nevertheless, I still agreed with the advisers about holding our fire, but on that Thursday evening I was extremely anxious and so agitated that I could not even sit down at home. My wife, Sheila, took me for a walk to Almscliffe Crag.[2] It was a glorious evening and I remembered how I had spent so many hours there as a boy, never dreaming that one day I would be standing admiring the wonderful view but with no joy in my heart.

As usual I woke up early the next day and, after patrolling the works, was in my office by 7.15am. At 7.30 my private line rang. It was Mr Robert Maxwell. He told me that his bid would be announced soon. Norton and Wright had recently announced their intention to change their name to Norton Opax. Maxwell said, 'Who are these people Norton Tampax? We can't have them interfering in our businesses. Waddingtons belongs with my British Printing and Communications Corporation. It is a great fit. You will have a place on the board. Together we can make a big impression on the packaging industry.' It sounded persuasive, but I told him that we did not need his help to beat Norton and Wright, that his intervention was unwelcome, and that we would resist all bids. (Later, on radio, I commented, 'I said two words to Mr Maxwell. I can't say on the air what the first word was, but the second word was "off".') Maxwell continued by saying that he knew that he had a bad reputation with some people, but that he was a good employer, and he would get some people that we both knew to phone me and explain that he was not so bad.

For a change, he was as good as his word. Before 10.00am I had calls from Olav Arnold of Arnolds (part of the Maxwell empire), Ken Petty of Petty's (part of the Maxwell empire) and Eric Tanzer, the managing director of Price Service, the UK's largest importers of printing machines and a big supplier to BPCC. I knew all three men well. Olav and I had been to Clare College and overlapped briefly. Ken and I were members of the same golf club. Eric was not a personal friend but I knew him well and respected him for his knowledge and dedication. He had come to England from Hungary to attend the London School of Printing and asked his father if he could stay on and start a branch of the family printing machines business in England.

---

2   Almscliffe Crag is in Wharfedale, near to North Rigton.

He became a naturalised British citizen in 1926. A Jew by birth, he became a Roman Catholic later on. He neither drank alcohol nor smoked, and he was a keep fit fanatic, yet he still seemed to belong to the printing trade, where such idiosyncrasies were unusual.

Ken, Olav and Eric all said that Maxwell was not so bad and hoped that we would join his group. They said that he interfered but had so much to do that the interference was only an occasional nuisance. I just laughed and said that I knew they didn't believe what they were saying but had to say it anyway because of Maxwell's power. The next day, Eric phoned me early to say, 'I could not sleep last night. I felt that I had perjured myself in suggesting that you cave in to Maxwell. He's a horrible man and you must resist with all the power at your disposal.' He quoted from Romeo and Juliet, Act 3, scene 1; 'A plague o' both your houses', meaning Norton Opax and BPCC. When I saw Eric by accident a few weeks later, he was in tears about it. Sheila and I took him and his wife Phyllis to Glyndebourne for years afterwards as a tribute to his steadfast support.

Well, if nothing else, this new development ended my worry of the previous evening. I knew that it gave us time to demonstrate our progress. And, as time went by, not only was our profit improving but we were able to report actual figures rather than make promises – a very telling factor. There were no biographies of Robert Maxwell at that time, but he was notorious. His affair with Leasco in 1969 triggered the Board of Trade enquiry led by two City of London heavyweights, Sir Ronald Leach and Mr Owen Stable QC. Their conclusion, which was to haunt Maxwell for the rest of his life, was 'We regret having to conclude that, notwithstanding Mr Maxwell's acknowledged abilities and energy, he is not in our opinion a person to be relied upon to exercise proper stewardship of a publicly quoted company'! I got a copy of the voluminous report and read it very thoroughly. I then had a much better understanding of the type of man we were dealing with. The best book about him is by Tom Bower and entitled *Maxwell the Outsider*. It tells the story of Jan Ludwig Hoch of the village of Solotvino Doly in Ruthenia, which was then part of Czechoslovakia and is now in the Ukraine. He left at the age of sixteen and found his way to England, where he joined the Pioneer Corps first of all and then managed a transfer to the North Staffs. Regiment. By the end of the war he was commissioned. He was highly intelligent with an excellent memory, a great facility for languages and boundless energy and self-confidence. During our bid, I checked up on his war record and was disappointed to discover that he really did reach the rank of captain and won the Military Cross because of outstanding bravery. After the war he was in

Berlin, attached to Intelligence as an interpreter and interrogator. It is said that he laid the foundations of his company Pergamon at that time. He acquired many scientific tracts for publication. Pergamon was a success due to his entrepreneurial flair, although he was involved in a business scandal even then, with one of his companies going under with losses to shareholders (including Harold MacMillan), while his private businesses prospered. Then, in 1969, he sold Pergamon to Saul Steinberg of Leasco with financial irregularities which led to the public humiliation which I mentioned above. He had been an MP since 1964. At the House of Commons he was the first and only MP to make his maiden speech at his first visit to the debating chamber and he soon earned the nickname 'The Bouncing Czech'.

But all this seemed to have no effect on the press, most of which admired him. Furthermore, there were plenty of people in the City of London who were prepared to do business with him. We were up against a formidable foe who had plenty of support.

Maxwell's first mistake was made at the start of his bid for Waddingtons. Either he was waiting to report his own profit figures or he had not planned his campaign. Anyway, he took far too long to follow up his announcement. From 17 June when he announced his bid, it took until 9 July for his offer document to be published – with a closing date of 2 August. This extra time was of great importance. A vital element of a bid defence is to have a united team. My slogan was: 'If the trumpet shall sound an uncertain note who will prepare for battle?' A common enemy unites the team, but it needed to be made clear that Maxwell was indeed an enemy and not a saviour. There were many on his side in spite of his chequered history. So, shortly after 17 June we had a meeting of managers and shop stewards (known as fathers of the chapel in the printing trade). I explained what had happened and what we might expect as the days went by. Then we answered questions. I had arranged for someone to ask, 'What would happen if Maxwell succeeded?' I replied, 'Well, let's ask David Perry who has worked for Maxwell.' David said that Maxwell would probably arrive by Rolls-Royce or helicopter, address the workforce, and say that Waddingtons was basically a good business but that the management had been poor and the investment insufficient. He would make promises to improve the management, invest in the company and bring new business, and he would declare that the future would be excellent. Then in a few months time he would insist on redundancies and wage cuts. From the back of the room someone spoke up; 'I am Eric Gill, the secretary of the local branch of SLADE, the union you all know and respect. I have never found myself in such agreement with a boss. I will tell you what happened to the process house T. and T. Gill here in Leeds not very long ago. Maxwell got control of the company. Just as Mr Perry says, he arrived by Rolls-Royce, and said that the company had been badly managed with insufficient investment but that he would correct that and bring new business. The eyes of the people present lit up, and a mood of confidence came over the company. Then, just a few weeks later, people arrived from BPCC headquarters to announce redundancies of half the workforce and a wage cut for the rest. I telephoned Mr Maxwell to say "Tell me this isn't true," and he said, "Things aren't as I thought they were when I addressed the workforce".' This intervention by Eric Gill galvanised those present. It confirmed their fears and doubts about Maxwell. From then on we had the employees on our side.

I have already mentioned our fundamental mistake. As soon as the first bid was announced, we should have sent out a clear and decisive message to the shareholders, telling them not to sell their shares as the bid was ludicrously low. We failed because we had insufficient confidence, and that went for our advisers too. They said at our first meeting in May that we could defend up to a price of 180p per share. In the end we beat off the bid of 284p, and fifteen months later the second bid was 500p per share. It is amazing how perceptions change as events unfold. At the start of our defence I think that some of our advisers thought that the idea was to get the best price for a weak and beleaguered company. Our plan was to repel the rapacious bidder.

We had excellent advisers. Kleinwort Benson, the merchant bank, and Cazenove, the broker, knew the company well and had stood by us through thick and thin. They had great reputations and they had both knowledge and know-how. Without Kleinworts and Cazenoves, Waddingtons could not have repelled the takeover bids. Hepworth and Chadwick, our local lawyers, were well up to dealing with the complexities of a takeover. And Kleinwort Benson also had on hand Herbert Smith, the excellent City of London corporate lawyers. What Hepworth and Chadwick could not deal with could be left to Herbert Smith with confidence. As for our accountants, we had Price Waterhouse, and thank goodness we had changed to them some years earlier. When Price Waterhouse signed off our financial forecasts they had credibility. We had Chris Bowes, our finance director, to thank for pushing through the change of auditors. In addition Chris had persuaded us that we should have a second bank just in case of conflict. How wise! A serious conflict did arise. Our long serving bank, NatWest, were also the bankers to the British Printing and Communication Group. BPCC, as it had become known, had been almost bankrupt and owed NatWest about £22 million. NatWest went to Robert Maxwell and put him into BPCC to try to save it, which he did. So there was no doubt about which side NatWest were on. Our local manager, John Tugwell, was on a course in the USA at the time. His stand-in, Trevor Skelley, never even spoke to us during the whole course of the bid. And although I knew a number of the very senior people at NatWest, (in 1978 I had spoken at their annual dinner), none of them phoned us to explain the dilemma and to wish us well. We were ignored. The other bank we had chosen was Midland. Whereas we dealt with NatWest on a local basis, our contact at Midland was Alan Hirst in London, and he was a very reliable ally. He was able to act quickly on his own authority. Yes, he proved to be a great friend when we needed him. We were only reasonably well served on the public relations front, but were unwilling to change horses with the enemy on the horizon. We had always cultivated the press and were well thought of, but at that time Maxwell was riding high. All the Sunday papers were solidly behind him. The others tended to side with him, especially *The Daily Telegraph*. Out of the national papers, only the *Financial Times* could be expected to be neutral, but they were on strike for almost the whole length of our battle. (They came into the fray with a vengeance in November 1984.) As for the *Yorkshire Post*, we started badly. Charles Pritchard, the business editor, spoke well of Richard Hanwell, the smooth managing director of Norton Opax. The newspaper described Hanwell as a committed Christian. A reporter asked me for my reaction. I said, 'Committed Christian – so were the members of the Spanish Inquisition.' Charles Pritchard seemed to be of the opinion that Waddingtons were doomed. It does not help to complain but on this occasion I did, rather off the cuff. It was at our local, the Windmill Inn in Linton, one Sunday evening. Gerry Holbrook, the managing director of the *Yorkshire Post*, came in and said something supportive. I said frostily that we intended to fight hard but that the *Yorkshire Post* seemed to be against us. Laughter from all. The next day Gerry saw to it that John Heffernan, the *Yorkshire Post's* City editor, was put on to the case. There was no doubt about John's allegiance, especially where Maxwell was concerned. His contempt for Maxwell was based on his knowledge of the Bouncing Czech's earlier business dealings. Why on earth so many journalists chose to ignore all that seedy past has always mystified me.

Another set of advisers need to be mentioned; Noble Lowndes, who dealt with our occupational pension plan. The pension fund became of great importance. We had had many redundancies with what seemed at the time to be good compensation. We had had vicious inflation. We had a rising stock market and a reduced workforce. Consequently, the pension fund had a very healthy surplus. We could reduce the annual contribution and enhance the profit. The pension advisers, along with many trade union leaders and politicians, seemed to think that the surplus belonged to the pension beneficiaries, and we had a hard job to explain to them that our final salary pension scheme was a contract between the company and its employees, and that the pension fund was there to see that the contract could be honoured. I asked the crucial question; if the surplus belongs to the employees, what if there is a deficit? Is it the responsibility of the employees to prop up the fund? Obviously not. The pension advisers' lack of understanding was not helpful.

WHITE KNIGHTS

'WHITE KNIGHTS' IS a term used to describe companies which apparently come to the rescue of those being attacked by ruthless predators. Often these so-called white knights are intent on the spoils of battle. They seek to gain advantage from a situation. Maxwell described himself as a white knight riding to save Waddingtons. I described him as a knight on an off-white charger. A *Guardian* newspaper reporter phoned me and said, 'I see that you have said that there are no white knights – only grey ones. What colour is Robert Maxwell?' I replied, 'It depends what light you see him in.'

During the bid of 1983 we never mentioned white knights and, strangely, we had few questions about them. We kept quiet about it afterwards as well. It would have seemed that we were not confident of victory. The fact is though that we were not confident, and it seemed to be sensible to examine all possibilities. I was the one with the most confidence but I was not as sure as I seemed to the outside world. Others in our senior team were even more uneasy about our chances of a successful defence. We had had a few years of poor performance and the memory of it all was not short.

We had white knights to choose from in the end. But to start with, Norman Gaunt looked for help among our US contacts, like International Paper, Mobil and Coors, all companies with which we had business connections. None showed interest. A merger and acquisitions specialist, William Cruise of New Jersey, approached others with no success. The general message was that Waddingtons packaging companies were jewels and that other parts, like the games division, could easily be sold. Bowater indicated that they were not interested. So did the Swedish packaging companies PLM and Esselte. I had talks with General Mills who owned Parker Brothers, along with other toy and games companies. Their executive could not see any situation except in terms of marketing. All they wanted was to get Monopoly for the UK. But I had already fought off General Mills' attempt to end our Monopoly licence by letting it be known that we would remove the very valuable Cluedo (Clue in the USA) licence and let their deadly competitors have it. They could not see that a generous offer for Waddingtons Games might be accepted and give their company an enormous opportunity for market domination and profit. Basically, their man couldn't thoil[3] to see another make a profit even if that meant a better profit for them.

One approach which we took very seriously came from the private company Linpac, the packaging empire of Evan Cornish. They approached us on 15 June 1983 before Maxwell's bid. They were not flush with cash and yet a cash bid was all that was open to them. However, they reckoned that parts of Waddingtons could be sold, leaving Linpac with a huge and successful packaging company. We met the talented sales chief, Harold Rogan, and also Martin Buckley, who eventually worked for Waddingtons. Linpac were very interested but we said that the price would have to be 250p and that was a bridge too far for them. The negotiations came to a halt.

On 13 July 1983 Smurfits approached us and we had useful discussions with Howard Kilroy, Michael Smurfit's operational chief, and also their merchant banker Morgan Grenfell, in the person of James Holt. Smurfit's plan was to sell part of their printing and packaging division in the UK to Waddingtons in return for shares, making Smurfit the holder of 30–35% of Waddingtons equity. This would let Smurfit concentrate on their major activity, which was corrugated packaging. The businesses involved were Thomas Preston (with three plants), Dobson and Crowther, Nobles, Brand Packaging and Sanderson and Clayton. It would have been difficult to implement all this though, as the 'rescue' would have been resisted strongly by the City and probably by most of our large shareholders. But as the offers rose and our share price rose as a result, the Smurfit plan evaporated.

Apart from an approach from a customer and friend John Syrad of British Vending Industries, the only other interesting possibility was put forward by Andrew Lauder, the managing director of Waddingtons Games Ltd. With the help of Hans Jani, the owner of the German playing card company Altenburg and Stralsunder, he proposed to buy the games company. He said that he wanted me to be the chairman, which would have made sense commercially but which I believe he suggested just to get me to agree.

---

3 'Thoil' is a Yorkshire word derived from the Saxon 'Thole', as in 'could not bear to see...'

Well, of course, they wanted it on the cheap while the parent company was beleaguered. Nothing came of it.

So in a nutshell, yes we welcomed the white knights, but it was a welcome tinged with suspicion and we never got anywhere near to a deal.

During the weeks that followed Maxwell's intervention, when it became apparent that the share price was so high that Norton Opax would not succeed,[4] we gained the contract for the supply of plastic containers to Van Den Berghs. It was huge. Of course, we wanted to announce it, but our customer said 'No'. The reason was that the impact on Metal Box, the other supplier, was so severe that the affair had to remain confidential. Our customer said that we could tell a select number of our major shareholders. This posed a dilemma. You are supposed to inform shareholders equally or not at all. But to keep silent might be to let the company go for too low a price, which was surely not in the shareholders' interest. We did visit many shareholders during July and generally found them favourably disposed towards us and, after a show of hesitation, we told them of the great Van Den Bergh's order for margarine containers.

During this middle period, our appeal to the Office of Fair Trading was rejected in spite of much support from employees, trade unions and MPs. It was the correct decision but we felt that if the takeover of Sotheby's could be blocked then anything might happen.

On 28 July we held our annual general meeting at noon at the works in Leeds. During the morning Mr Maxwell phoned me, urging once again that I should meet him to negotiate an agreed bid. He threatened me by saying that if our resistance continued he would not be feeling so well disposed towards us when he won control. I said that there was nothing to negotiate as the company was not for sale. Maxwell sent our friend Ken Petty to the AGM in order to ask some awkward questions. On arrival Ken told us what the questions were to be. There was no doubt about Ken's loyalty to us. Then at the meeting when it was time for questions on the report and accounts, Ken stood up and I said, 'Are you a shareholder?'

'No,' he said, 'I'm representing Mr Maxwell and BPCC.'

'Well,' I said, 'Have you a letter of authority?'

'No.'

'Well you can't speak or ask a question' (stunned silence) '– but,' I continued, 'as you are a friend, carry on.' We answered the questions and then Ken said that he hoped that Waddingtons would win, and I invited him

---

4 Norton Opax withdrew from the bidding soon after.

to stay for a drink after the meeting. The assembled advisers thought it was very droll.

I have mentioned Mr Maxwell's attempts to get us to meet him. We refused from the start, although David Perry and I did meet him on one occasion. Such meetings can so easily be misrepresented and misunderstood. If our employees had known that I had met Mr Maxwell, they might have suspected that I was making an agreement with him. People on the shop floor, even those who trust their senior managers, are always anxious that the bosses might be cooking something up between them. Maxwell would have called a press conference, and in those plummy tones of his would have said something along the lines of: 'Mr Watson and Mr Perry and I have had a very fruitful meeting. We are agreed that there will be great synergy in the merging of BPCC and Waddingtons. I am happy to confirm that both Mr Watson and Mr Perry will have senior positions in our new enlarged enterprise, etc., etc.', and the workforce and many of the gullible press would have said, 'Its all over. They've caved in.'

Ignoring our own rule, we met Maxwell because he indicated that he wanted to withdraw from the battle and needed to speak to us about it. It turned out to be a hoax. He wanted to cajole us and then, when that failed, threaten us. As we left, both David and I felt that there was a powerful magnetism about the man that made us almost want to agree with him.

Then, in August, things warmed up.

On 1 August BPCC increased their offer, the cash alternative being 250p, and then proceeded to pay Norton Opax a very healthy 275.6p per share for part of their holding, which brought the BPCC share holding in Waddingtons up to nearly 15%. This was an important figure. The Takeover Panel rules decree that if the bidder buys over 15% of the shares, then all shareholders must be offered the highest price paid. At this stage our financial advisers thought that we had had it. But there was still plenty of excitement to come.

First, Mr Maxwell quoted one of our former senior employees out of context, and we had a field day correcting his error. It was a mistake made because of lack of care on his part. It had the effect of further undermining his credibility. Then came an innovation in the history of takeovers. During the weekend of 12 and 13 August, I was wrestling with a problem. I quote from my notes of the board meeting we held on the Saturday afternoon: 'Went through the proof of the letter to shareholders. Main issues thrashed out again. A) We decide not to refer to Mr Maxwell's record. B) We decide to carry on knocking BPCC shares. Problem here is that shareholders may say to themselves, "the cash offer closes before the share offer; if I do not take the cash and BPCC win I'm stuck with the BPCC shares. Therefore play safe and take the cash." The more we knock the BPCC shares, the more apprehensive we make the shareholders.'

By Sunday evening I had an idea which I put to our merchant banker. I intended to visit the major shareholders to say to them, 'I believe that a majority will reject the BPCC bid. However, unless the shareholders know this some of them may play safe and accept the cash offer, which closes before the share offer. Therefore, I ask you: if you intend to reject the offer, will you allow me to tell the other major shareholders and, if enough support is gathered, will you allow me to announce it publicly?' Our merchant banker said that it was most unusual, had never been done before and was a long shot, but that it was worth trying.

I set out on Monday morning: I remember it well because it was one of the hottest days of that summer, and my mission was one of the most important selling jobs I have ever had to do. My first call was on the Britannic Assurance Company in Birmingham. They had been Waddingtons' largest shareholder for many years. They had about 300 companies in their portfolio and kept in touch with them all. I used to visit the chief investment manager, Frank Weavers, every two years and he would visit us in the other years. I remember well that after a year or two I said, 'I wish that you would call me Victor', and he replied, 'Of course. Call me Frank. But I agree with you that it is presumptuous to get on to first name terms too early.' I had summed him up correctly. He was a man of strong principles, very fair in his dealings and with an eye for the truth, not an uncommon feature when it came to financial affairs. Whatever the state of the company we had to be straight with him, and we had to be careful not to tell him anything which made him an insider because then he would refuse to buy or sell Waddingtons shares. So when I reached his office, I was greeted as an old friend who was in trouble and needed help. But it was not just Frank's decision. He took me into lunch where the chairman and his fellow directors listened to my descriptions of the state of the bid, the future, the horror we felt at the thought of Maxwell owning the company and my plan for a statement of intent from major shareholders. Their concern was that as stewards of other people's money, they had a duty of care and could not decide in our favour just because they sympathised with us. They had a duty to follow the best course financially, regardless of the effect on people. So the arguments for and against went on through lunch, all very civilised and serious. Frank kept quiet. Then at last he spoke to his colleagues in words like this. 'We have been investors in Waddingtons for a long time. We have been treated by

Victor as an owner of the business. We have been kept informed. The relationship has been excellent. We are in fact partners. We owe a duty to Victor and his colleagues. We will not be criticised for showing our colours, for siding with the underdog, for standing in the way of a man who has been named as unfit to be the steward of shareholders' funds. I strongly believe that we should agree to the proposal that we decide here and now not to accept the bid and allow Waddingtons to publish the decision.' Almost at once they agreed. I stopped any more persuasion and got on my way as soon as possible, with the thought in my mind 'A friend in need is a friend indeed.'

At 2.30pm I left the building, went out into the tremendously hot day and drove down the motorway to the nearest service station where I got into a phone box and first of all telephoned Gordon Craig of M and G. He soon agreed to the plan. I then phoned Anthony Forbes of Cazenoves and asked him to tee up meetings with the others, having first of all explained the plan. Next, I contacted John McArthur of Kleinworts, told him of my success and asked him to begin work on further necessary details. I then called David Perry and asked him to get on with phoning some of the others, and I asked Peter Stephens to do the family ones.

My diary note says:

Perspiring and uncomfortable but confidence improving. As I drove down the motorway it certainly seemed to me to be senseless to drive all the way to London, so I ditched the car at Rugby and took the train down to Euston. From the company flat I phoned various small shareholders to find out how they stood. They were grateful for the call but of course some of them involved considerable conversation. In the case of my step Great Aunt Dodie for instance, I had to hear all about the sale of the house, or the lack of the sale of the house, and all about Trethowan's wedding up in Middlesbrough. That evening I felt tremendously worked up and really tired out and wondered what on earth to do and suddenly had the bright idea of calling at Tiberios for dinner where they have a good pianist, and my word it really did the trick to sit there, have the occasional chat with the pianist and listen to his marvellous playing.

Later on I went down to Burrup and Matthiesons in the hope of seeing our rejection document being printed. Keith Petty, the night manager, met me. Evidently he is a distant relation of the Leeds Pettys. I was shown into a room and given a drink and then Marc Cramsie and Chris Kirkness of Kleinworts arrived, wearing jeans of course, and looking exactly like a couple of Sloane rangers. They got down to the checking job and after a drink I left because Keith Petty wouldn't let me in because there was so much sensitive stuff being printed. I walked back to the flat crossing Blackfriars bridge, it was a balmy evening and all London was beautiful. No wonder it inspired songsmiths like Hubert Gregg, Noel Coward and many others. I couldn't help thinking of Wordsworth's poem – 'Earth has not anything to show more fair, dull would he be of soul who could pass by a sight so touching in its majesty.' Even though those lines were written on Westminster bridge, Blackfriars bridge was just as exciting at night. At the far end was the Unilever building looking exactly like a great big book end. As I walked along I noticed how easy it would be to jump in; the parapet was even lower than the fence into the road, easier to jump into the river than into the road, and probably safer too, but anyway I didn't feel like jumping in, I was beginning to feel that we were on the way to victory.

The next day we all worked furiously to persuade the other shareholders to agree to the plan. Roy Dearden of Cazenoves was a great help and so was Martin Bailey of Stock Beech, the broker in Bristol, who had been very helpful and introduced Gordon Craig of M and G, a very loyal shareholder. During the day the Takeover Panel agreed that we could release the figure of the shareholders not accepting the bid, providing that we gave them a list of those shareholders.

The following day we captured a few more shareholders, including Rothschilds. It was not all success of course. I called on David Liss of the fund manager called Target. They occupied that new building near to where Prunier's used to be in St James Street – the building that looks as if it has been made of dustbins – new dustbins of course – they're very particular in St James Street. They had a small room on the third floor, just four or five chaps, screens and phones, all very slick and businesslike. David Liss told me that they had bought the Waddingtons shares for a self-employed pension fund. He had bought just after the Norton and Wright bid as a 'situation', as he put it. He said he was a weak hold. He said that our defence had been excellent. He sympathised with us, but he said that he had to perform for the fund and if that meant selling or accepting then he would have to do it.

We met in Lord Rockley's room at Kleinworts to review the acceptances and to hammer out a statement. It all proved to be immensely difficult. Frank Weavers had gone on holiday. His alternate wanted time to consider the statement. M and G's Gordon Craig was away and I spoke to his boss, David Tucker, who was very stuffy about it all and didn't want to do it. He was still smarting from a smear in *The Mail on Sunday* and thought that they would be in the spotlight. In the end Roy Dearden persuaded David Tucker, but only after more problems with the proposed statement. Britannic liked paragraph one but not paragraph two. M and G like paragraph two but not paragraph one. Then Singer and Friedlander, representing Watmoughs, said that they would not be included. Exasperated, I phoned Patrick Walker, Watmoughs boss. He said that they did not want to be long-term holders and could we find a buyer. I said, 'It's impossible to find a buyer for such a large holding. Look, we've got a lot of people on our side, we're going to win. Come with us. Be on our side. Don't be branded as the firm which let Waddingtons down.' Later on we got a message from Singer and Friedlander that Watmoughs were in.

The press statement that we issued on Wednesday, 17 August was as follows:

JOHN WADDINGTON PLC

> Waddingtons announce that shareholders in Waddingtons holding in aggregate 46.2% of the issued ordinary share capital have indicated that it is their present intention not to accept the BPCC offers.
>
> The Board of Waddingtons concludes, therefore, that this firm expression of support from a number of important shareholders underlines the Board's strong advice to all shareholders who have not yet made a decision that they should <u>not accept</u> the BPCC offers.

The press came on one after another. 46.2% of the shareholders was almost a knockout. Of the large shareholders only Norwich Union, Guardian Royal Exchange and Scottish Amicable were unhelpful.

At the end of a hot, exhausting but also exhilarating day, we went for a beer at The Lamb in Leadenhall Market. It was about the best I ever tasted.

Private or individual shareholders can be of great importance. They are often more loyal to the company, which they have come to think of as their own. Sometimes there is the local factor to consider; the company belongs to the locality and if it is taken over the decisions will be made elsewhere. Rowntrees is perhaps the best British example. Yes, Nestlé have invested in the York factory but the heart and soul of the business is no longer anywhere near to York. Those who work at the York factory do not have the same feeling of loyalty that they had when the decisions affecting the future of the business were made in the same place that they worked in. The workers are more likely to think of themselves as wage-slaves than as members of a great enterprise.

Also, it has to be said that private shareholders are often apathetic, more likely to leave things as they are. Some do not even know what is going on and never return the documents. One elderly lady, a large Waddingtons shareholder, was most definitely not in that category though. Her name was Mrs Driscoll. Before the bid we had never noticed that this shareholder in Essex had 44,000 shares. It was a small fortune in 1983. Early on in the bid I decided to give her a ring, just to say that we were resisting strongly and to hang on and to ask if she wanted any advice. I could not find her in the phone book and Directory Enquiries said that she appeared to have no telephone. So I wrote to her. Next morning I received a call from her daughter. 'I'm calling from next door,' she said, 'My mother and I are not on the phone. It seems so expensive. My mother says, don't worry, she'll not sell the shares or accept Mr Maxwell's bid, she doesn't like him anyway. She's had the shares for an awfully long time and they have grown enormously and paid out lots in dividends and she is grateful.' We conversed for a while but I resisted the temptation to ask how Mrs Driscoll, who didn't have a telephone and thought of herself as poor, should have come by the shares in the first place. Many weeks later we learned the answer. It was August, and the dénouement was at hand. We were telephoning and visiting shareholders, all those with 500 or more shares. Peter Stephens, our company secretary, did a trawl through East Anglia. By strange coincidence, while Peter was there talking with Mrs Driscoll, they popped in from next door to say that Mr Maxwell's representative was on the phone to speak with her. Goodness knows how they found the telephone number! It turned out that Mrs Driscoll had been the maid of Frederick Eley, the chairman of the board of Waddingtons way back in 1913 when the company was insolvent and my grandfather was made general manager. Frederick Eley was the manager of the National Provincial Bank in Leeds and he was also a shareholder in Waddingtons. The bank, under Mr Eley's guidance, continued to support Waddingtons. Such a procedure would be against the law these days and may have been classed as coffee house tricks then, but it worked. Waddingtons was saved, including the jobs, the creditors' money and the shareholders' investments. Mr Eley gave his maid a few shares in Waddingtons, saying 'Keep those for your old age. They will grow in value.' And how right he was! They were one of the sparkling stocks of their day. Mrs Driscoll's loyalty was rewarded. By the late summer of 1984 the shares were worth £5 apiece, and the dividend was rising again.

In passing, it is worth recording that we never threw mud at Maxwell and I always referred to him as Mr Maxwell. Many of our conservative shareholders like Britannic Assurance would have disliked a slanging match, and we had to recognise that all the Sunday papers supported Maxwell, and some of the dailies were favourable to him, and the *Financial Times* was on strike.

It is also worth recording that when Simon Barrow of Kleinworts went on holiday, his boss John McArthur took over and he was a bonny fighter, determined to win. His ethical stance was that winning was best for everybody and it was no use sticking to the Queensbury rules: 'If you lose, you lose. There's no appeal. You'll get no prizes for being decent!'

The final period really began on 1 August with Mr Maxwell's final offer amounting to 250p in cash, or 278p on a valuation of the BPCC shares. The offer was described as 'FINAL', and this was a blunder. It was, of course, an attempt to hurry things along – 'Buy now while stocks last'. With the permitted extensions we knew it could only go on until 7 September, but now the offer could not be increased. BPCC tried to wriggle out of its self-imposed straightjacket by proposing to increase its dividend, but the Takeover Panel would not allow it.

This was the time when Maxwell made some inaccurate statements which gave us some publicity mileage. Maxwell was using all his best efforts to get shareholders to accept and his people even made the mistake of telephoning our directors' wives to make exaggerated claims, which caused yet more adverse publicity for BPCC. We were also engaged in the struggle for people's minds. Every shareholder with over 500 shares was visited or telephoned. One large shareholder, the Norwich Union, had accepted the BPCC offer. I had been told by our brokers that the Norwich Union would not see representatives of either side. We had been told this from the start. We made a mistake in accepting the advice. As late as 24 August I got to work on it. I was spurred on by the announcement that Mr Maxwell had 45.85% acceptances and by the near certainty that a major party in our 46.2% must have defected to the other side. I telephoned the investment manager at the Norwich Union. It was a difficult call. He did not want to see me. I said that I had some information which was commercially confidential but which would make them reconsider. I insisted that it was my duty to see him and also insisted that it was his duty to see me. Eventually he agreed and David Perry and I set off in order to be there at 9.00am the next morning. We were greeted politely but told that if we imparted any information which he considered to be such that he was placed in a privileged position, he would exclude himself from the decision taking. We did in fact tell him privileged information but explained the rationale. David was on top form and with John McArthur corroborating our story we persuaded

Norwich Union to change their minds, which was a very courageous thing for them to do. We had other successes at the same time and were able to announce significant withdrawals.

The bidder always tries to get the bandwagon rolling and our sole purpose was to stop the bandwagon in its tracks. With the famous 46.2% and then the significant withdrawals, we were on the offensive and Maxwell even conceded in a TV interview that Mr Watson had 'thrown him a googly,' to use his own words.

During the Bank Holiday weekend we thought of another salvo to fire in to the BPCC flank. Early in August the press published a story about Mr Maxwell's coup in making a £20 million deal to develop a site in Watford together with Sainsbury's. The *Evening Standard* in London said, 'The BPCC share price was helped by confirmation of just what a brilliant deal Mr Maxwell has done over the Odhams' site at Watford.' Shortly afterwards a BPCC offer document to the Waddingtons' shareholders mentioned the site, but without the figure of £20 million. If the figure had been mentioned, it would have had to be audited in order to comply with the Takeover Panel rules. We recognised it as a clever device – the idea of the £20 million had been clearly planted in people's minds. We were suspicious and we set about investigating it very thoroughly. By Thursday 1 September, we were able to put out a devastating press release exposing the misleading impression, which I followed up by telephoning all the main newspapers. That night was one of the worst for me. I had several other things of great concern on my mind, plus the fear that our accusation about the Watford site would backfire. Then we heard that a Korean airliner had been shot down by the Russians, and for me it was almost the last straw. I tried to go for a walk, but could not. Even Mozart could not soothe the nerves.

Next morning, however, we learned that we had scored a direct hit. The *Financial Times* (now back in circulation) carried a long story quoting a Watford Council official. 'The council has been against out-of-town-centre shopping complexes because of the detrimental effect on the town centre and Mr Maxwell has been perfectly well aware of that fact.'

I am sure that we well and truly aggravated Maxwell this time. On Sunday 5 September he was interviewed by David Frost on breakfast television. When Frost asked him, 'If you won would you keep the managing director who's fought so hard against you?', Maxwell replied, 'I never believe in selling the skin of the rabbit before I've caught it.'

From mid-August it was possible by the Stock Exchange rules for those shareholders who had accepted the bid to withdraw their acceptance. Our major success was the Norwich Union with 4.2% of the shares, but there were others to be tackled. We considered finding people to buy shares from those who had accepted and then withdrawing the acceptance. I should reiterate that this was in mid-August. It was not an easy task. But one day in my office I was sitting at my table and David Perry was leaning on my side table and he said, 'What about some of your business friends?' 'Of course', I replied. We'd considered this early on but then it had slipped my mind. 'I'll start at once.' I telephoned Neil Pullan, an old friend and the son-in-law of one of my father's best friends. I explained the situation briefly. Neil just said, 'Well, I have funds on deposit and it's at your disposal.'

'I'll come round now and go into detail', I said.

'No,' he replied, 'no need for that. Just tell me who the certified cheque is to be made out to and you can have it this afternoon.' It involved seven figures. I think that it is the most remarkable thing that anybody has ever said to me. True to his word we got the cheque and did a deal with Scottish Amicable, who had indicated that they would accept an offer. My brother John drove to Glasgow and next morning the deal was done and a withdrawal of the bid notice posted at the Stock Exchange within hours. My next-door neighbour, Peter Asquith, came up trumps too and that was another withdrawal (a smaller one – Jupiter Asset Management). Maxwell was trying to announce further acceptances as if he had a bandwagon rolling. But we were posting defections from his side to ours and stopping that wagon.

A new shareholder had appeared, to wit, Philips and Drew. I found out the name of the fund manager. It was Bill Horwood and I went to see him. He listened to my tale but he was noticeably uncomfortable and said very little. But he said that I could see him again a week later if anything developed. When I saw him a week later, he spoke out. 'I'm in a difficult position', he said. 'I bought shares in Waddingtons not long ago on behalf of the pension funds of both Gallaghers and Woolworths, and I told them that my aim was to accept the bid and end up with BPCC shares. Then you came along and suddenly it isn't a faceless transaction any more. Instead of just a financial affair you introduced the personal aspect. You made me sympathetic and I regret what I've done now.' Well, we talked it over and in the end he agreed that we could talk directly to Gallaghers and Woolworths to see if we could persuade them to instruct Philips and Drew to withdraw their acceptance of the bid. We succeeded with Woolworths, largely because of the chairman, William Beckett.

The intense activity continued for the last few days, and we even got a shareholder to withdraw on the very last day. At 3.40pm on 7 September,

Mr Maxwell himself telephoned me – yes, give him his due – to say, 'I concede defeat'.

And so ended a fearful struggle of which the saddest part concerned a defecting friend. Part of the famous 46.2% was the 310,000 shares owned by Watmoughs, the Bradford printers. They went over to the other side so that at the end, of the 42% which Maxwell had on his side, 24% was made up of his own holding and those of Norton Opax and Watmoughs. An alliance of unfriendly printers against Waddingtons. Both Norton Opax and Watmoughs turned the knife in the wound after the bid failed by selling their shares to Maxwell.

FOOTNOTE TO THE 1983 BID

Many shares are held in pseudonyms known as nominees. Some are foreign and not all that straightforward to detect. But most companies examine their share registers and discover the identities of the true owners. This register has to be made available to a bidder on payment of a small fee. Maxwell's lot had been sent such a register at the start of the bid but during August 1983 they suddenly realised that many shares had new owners and the register needed to be examined again. They requested a copy from us.

We delayed sending them a copy. Our finance director, Chris Bowes, even said to them that he'd mistakenly filed it under 'e' for important papers. But in the meantime they had found out that we could not refuse to let them see the register at our premises. Maxwell sent Olav Arnold to see it. It was unkind and tactless as Olav was a personal friend, but we had to deal with him nevertheless. He arrived with a secretary and a notebook. We said, 'The law says that you can look at the register. No secretary. No notebook. We'll stand over you while you just look at the register.' Well, there was too much information to absorb, so Olav went away with very little. Then they sent Ken Petty in the afternoon. We knew that he would have been given some specific items to examine and report back on. So we prepared a different ruse. We placed the register in a room far removed from the front door where he arrived; getting to it involved a walk through the works which Ken had never seen and which we knew he would find interesting. Then, on his way back, we listened for his arrival along the corridor and in turn came out to pass the time of day with him. I was the last, and he said straight away, 'You buggers. I can't remember a thing because of all this gossiping.'

Later on, but only after Maxwell's lot had gone to Court, we delivered a copy of the register to Arnolds, one of the Leeds subsidiaries of BPCC. A few days after the bid battle had ended, Peter Stephens came to me with a brown paper parcel. 'What do you think of this?' he asked. I looked at it. Inside the parcel was a thick envelope and inside that was our shareholders' register. The envelope was addressed to Robert Maxwell at Maxwell House, Worship Street, London and was marked that the stamp on it was insufficient. The Maxwell underlings had refused to pay the extra, no doubt following company policy, and the envelope had been 'returned to sender' – us. It shows how the plans and schemes of the mighty may so easily be frustrated by the actions of the minions.

A painting of Victor Watson by Frank Salisbury in 1943, just before he died.

Norman Watson, Master of the Worshipful Company of Makers of Playing Cards.

Douglas Brearley: Director of John Waddingtons Ltd, and writer of the early history.

Beric Watson, Managing Director of Waddingtons Games Ltd.

THE WADDINGTONS STORY

Victor H Watson, MA
Chairman

W Anthony B Brown,
MA, CEng, FIMechE
*Deputy Chairman
Director, Baker
Perkins Holdings PLC*

David G Perry
Managing Director

Kenneth Lunn
*Assistant Managing
Director*

Christopher J L Bowes,
BA, FCA, FCMA, JDipMA
Finance Director

Michael D Abrahams
*Non-executive
Chairman, Weavercraft
Carpets Ltd
Director, Prudential
Corporation PLC*

John G B Watson MP

Peter B Stephens,
BA, FCA
Secretary

Above: All the Waddingtons directors at the time of Maxwell's second bid. (Board of directors in 1984.)

Left: Victor Watson and Sir Ken Morrison at the University of Leeds, 29 April 2004. Victor has just presented Sir Ken for his honorary degree.

Victor Watson Jnr. playing and singing with his grandson Fergus.

David Perry, Chairman of Waddingtons, with HM the Queen.

The iconic Waddingtons factory, Wakefield Road, Leeds.

Norman Watson at his desk in 1960.

Peter Stephens' Retirement Party, 1987

Back row (l–r): Andrew Dalton, Keith Rawcliffe (Price Waterhouse), Peter Shakeshaft, Michael Abrahams, Chris Tuffs (NatWest), John Jorgensen, Tony Brown, Chris Bowes, Arthur Stone (Leeds and Holbeck Building Society), Martin Buckley, Marten Fraser (Price Waterhouse), Geoff Walker (Bain Dawes), Kenn Lunn, John Turner (Bain Dawes), Peter Honeysett (NatWest), Desmond Brashier (Noble Lowndes), Callum McCarthy (Kleinwort Benson), Dennis Thoy (Noble Lowndes), Alan Hirst (Midland Bank), David Sykes (Hepworth and Chadwick), Jonathon Guest (Hepworth and Chadwick), John Watson, Geoff Gibson, Roy Dearden (Cazenove), The Hon. Philip Remnant (Kleinwort Benson).

Front row (l–r): Doug Brearley, Norris Hodgson, Peter Stephens, Victor Watson, Everard Chadwick, Ted Rundle.

CHAPTER TWELVE

MAXWELL'S BID OF 1984

THE FIRST ROUND of the fight against Robert Maxwell ended on 7 September 1983 when the BPCC bid for Waddingtons was beaten off. In admitting defeat Maxwell also called for board representation at Waddingtons. It was a clever ploy. Instead of saying to us, 'Well done', the press asked, 'What is your response to Mr Maxwell?' They seemed to think that it was a reasonable request. We said that it would be like having Rupert Murdoch on the board of the *Daily Mirror*.

Maxwell also lost no time in mopping up the available Waddingtons shares. He bought those of Norton Opax and Watmoughs and by 10 October 1983 had 29.9%. He had to stop there of course because he would have had to bid if he had acquired more shares and he was prohibited by the Takeover Panel rules from bidding for a year from 7 September 1983.

Maxwell also wrote a letter to the Waddingtons shareholders which was never despatched. *The Daily Telegraph* of 28 September reported that the letter included the phrase, 'Let us work together to keep the management on its toes.' We waited for the letter to arrive. It did not. Michael Beckett of the *Telegraph* was adamant that the letter had been released to him. Maxwell's advisers denied its existence. Presumably Maxwell had decided to do it and then been persuaded by his advisers that it should not be done. It was an indication of how he worked and also an indication that he intended to bid for Waddingtons again when the time was ripe.

At Waddingtons, we did not stand still. We were doing well. The share price was higher than it would have been without the bid. We looked for companies to buy, the aim being to enhance our market position and at the same time reduce Maxwell's percentage of the shares. Our intention was to make ourselves a more desirable acquisition but at the same time a more unattainable one. We acquired Vickers Business Forms and the House of

Questa, one of our competitors in the field of postage stamp printing. To pay for Questa we initiated a rights issue. This move did not meet with the approval of all of our advisers, but we were determined to be on the offensive and not be afraid of what Maxwell might do.

As an example of our plotting, here are my notes of a meeting held in London on 22 March 1984 to consider Waddingtons' strategy:

Present: Messrs J. McArthur) Kleinwort Benson
S. Barrow)

Messrs W. A. B. Brown)
M. D. Abrahams)
D. G. Perry) Waddingtons
J. G. B. Watson)
V. H. Watson)

John McArthur said that in his opinion Maxwell will bid again as soon as he is entitled to. He thought that by that time (with the help of friends) he might well have added to his holding, taking him above the 30%, even though such action would be against the rules. He said that in any case Maxwell will have such a start that he will be in a very good position to win.

Michael Abrahams said that it was vital that we should not let the company go to Maxwell. He said that defensive strategies would not work and the only way to remain independent would be to get Waddingtons re-rated by the City. This would entail doing such things as giving the company a go-go image. The first essential would be to sell the games companies; the second would be to invest in new, more exciting things.

Simon Barrow said that Waddingtons was quite highly rated already at a fully taxed P/E of 15. He said that new exciting things are not so easy to find as everybody was looking for them, and while not disagreeing with the plan if it could be made to work, seemed to favour conversations with possible white knights.

It seemed to be generally agreed that it would be possible to have conversations with potential white knights without whetting their appetites so much that they would want to bid anyway.

VHW asked this question; 'If we sell our games companies, will people say "Whatever are Waddingtons thinking of – selling their birthright, selling the things they are best known for?"' John McArthur and Michael Abrahams said that people would definitely not say such a thing.

John Watson asked this question: 'With our recent acquisition of Vickers Business Forms, with our successes with plastics, with the story about polyester trays in the USA, with our acquisition of Questa and success with postage stamps and with our adhesive label project, have we got enough exciting things going without such drastic action as selling the games companies?' John McArthur and Michael Abrahams said that we had definitely not got enough with that package to give ourselves the fire power to resist Maxwell.

John McArthur and Simon Barrow said that Waddingtons cannot afford to launch unwelcome takeover bids. There is always the risk of failure for Waddingtons. We would lose a whole lot of emotional support.

Simon Barrow agreed with VHW's comment in his report that Waddingtons needs to be much more than twice its size in order to deter Maxwell. John McArthur and Michael Abrahams disagreed with that view and pointed out that it is the quality, not the size, that matters.

It was agreed that David Perry and VHW would try to construct a plan to sell the games companies and invest elsewhere. The implication was that if a plan which is workable cannot be constructed, then we should sell out rather than fight Maxwell and probably lose. There was some discussion as to selling out or merging. A three-way merger was dismissed as too complex in the time available and a number of possible white knights or grey knights were discussed. VHW found himself trying to decide whether it is better to sell the lot rather than sell off the games companies anyway.

SINCE THE MEETING

Since the meeting VHW has asked Beric Watson to think about the possible sale of the games companies.

Since the meeting David Perry and VHW have asked Phillip Brain to work on ideas for development in plastics in the USA.

OTHER PLANS FOR GAMES

VHW has tried to think about what else we could do, such as making a deal with someone like Spears or Hestair. If a larger, amalgamated company did ensue, there would be no cash for Waddingtons and we would have the problem of losing the contribution from games. We might have a shareholding in the larger games company instead but unless the enlarged games company was manifestly better placed then we would still have the supposed disadvantage of a stake in games but with no control. It raises the question of which is more important; just to get rid of the games companies or to raise some cash for investment in further ventures.

SALE OF THE GAMES COMPANIES

The possible purchasers could be:

> *General Mills*
> *Milton Bradley*
> *CBS*
> *David Yea (who owns Matchbox Toys)*
> *Fisher Price*
> *Mattel*
> *Hasbro*

The big question is whether or not they would pay a price which would compensate us sufficiently to ease the pain of losing the large contribution. VHW has asked Simon Barrow what he thinks will be the maximum price we would receive. We must remember that the information that Monopoly may be lost will have an adverse effect on the value of the business (as it will on the contribution as well). It would seem to VHW that we would be doing very well to get £8 million for the two companies and the contribution lost on the current year's trading would be £1,470,000. If we had another profitable venture ready and needed the money, then it might be a different story. VHW has asked Ken Lunn how much of the central costs could be saved if we disposed of the games business and he has promised to look at it, but a first impression is that it would be difficult to save a large amount.

Any money raised above book value might give rise to capital gains tax, thus reducing the benefit. It might be possible to eliminate this by hanging on to the rights of a game like Cluedo and continuing to receive royalties. This would also have the effect of reducing the price that we would expect someone to pay but on the other hand it might be just that one property which is what excites a potential buyer.

AN INTERMEDIATE PLAN

In spite of the reservations of John McArthur and Michael Abrahams, VHW feels that the following might make a good, positive story for the City:

1) Acquire Questa and get the stamp contract.
2) Acquire a UK plastics business.
3) Prepare for the launch of the adhesive labels project with maximum impact on the City.
4) Prepare for the purchase of a plastics business or businesses in the USA coupled with the exploitation of our Polyester Terephthalate (PET) tray technology.
5) Conduct a publicity campaign to extol the virtues of the new-look Waddingtons.

We can give a strong impression of a company really on the move. It leaves us with the question of the games companies. We could sell the Canadian company and then we could say that our games involvement is down to, say, 10% of total sales and cash is being generated. The disadvantage of this is that it might reduce the saleability of the UK games company. Alternatively, we could have a go at trying to sell the two games companies for a really satisfactory price but the disadvantage of this is that there is a risk of the attempted sale becoming public knowledge and yet the chances of success are small.

THE PLAN THAT VHW FAVOURS

1. Get Questa (for shares).
2. Acquire another UK company, possibly in plastic packaging (for shares).
3. Acquire a USA plastics business or businesses.
4. Publicity campaign.
5. Commence tentative talks with a few white knights with the following criteria:
   a) Unlikely to bid without our agreement.
   b) Large enough; market capitalization in excess of £100 million.
   c) Compatible style of management.
   d) Strategic reasons for the acquisition of Waddingtons.
   e) The temperament for a fight.

VHW, 28 March 1984.

On 21 June 1984 Ansbacher, Maxwell's merchant bank, told Kleinwort Benson that Maxwell was ready to dispose of his holding in Waddingtons. Cazenoves said that it would be impossible to place such a large block, particularly during the run up to the rights issue. Ansbacher wrote on 13 July demanding board representation for Maxwell or else they would vote against the rights issue and other resolutions at the annual general meeting and also sell their shares. This was the very day that Maxwell bought the *Daily Mirror* for £113.4 million, an amazing exploit which included an unusual piece of cinema verité with Clive Thornton, the *Daily Mirror* chief, hearing the bad news live in front of the cameras.

Our annual general meeting was held in London for the first time, at the Connaught Rooms. We thought that more of our large shareholders would attend if it was in London and we wanted to take the fight to the enemy. The courteous George Willett, a retired partner of Grieveson Grant, represented Maxwell and before the meeting he told me that he intended to demand a poll. We were ready of course with all the advisers lined up. But I was not ready for Mr Willett who came up to me at the table after I had called for a poll and said, 'There seems to have been a bit of a cock-up. I see that we have voted for Resolution Number Three and against Resolution Number Four, and it should be the other way round.' Thereupon he changed the vote, which meant that they blocked a change in the articles but allowed the allotment of shares for cash which, in the short term, was more helpful. This was yet another example of the confusion that existed on the other side. Maxwell was brilliant but also erratic. My colleague David Perry summed him up well as a misguided missile.

At the meeting another dissident shareholder, Lonrho, voted against everything. Lonrho had become shareholders during the first bid. David Perry and I had called on them. We met Robin Whitten, a director, who assured us that the shares were just a trade investment. But after a while the door opened and the famous Tiny Rowland himself appeared. He fixed us with those penetrating eyes and told us that their holding was strategic.

The rights issue went ahead. The Maxwell companies appeared not to take up their entitlement. Five months later, our defence document read, 'We have now ascertained, after encountering considerable delays on the part of those involved, that, far from allowing its percentage holding in Waddingtons to fall after the rights issue, an associate of the Pergamon Group, Pergamon Press Inc., through an American brokerage house, acquired on 9 August 1984 165,000 of the 375,000 Ordinary Shares the Pergamon Group was entitled to. This acquisition was not formally disclosed until after the current bid was announced. The balance was sold to a subsidiary of Lonrho plc.' It was a blatant breach of the Stock Exchange rules. There was no disciplinary action. One wonders why the rules are put in place at all.

The final bid of 1983 was 276p. The 'rights' price in 1984 was 375p. By mid-October the price of Waddingtons shares was 450p. Desultory discussions about the placing of Maxwell's shares had been going on, but we knew from internal sources that a bid was planned. On 24 October Kleinworts withdrew the offer to help to place the shares. That evening Maxwell phoned to say that he was going to bid. He suggested that we meet to discuss it but I refused. (A short while later we were both at the Printers' Charitable Corporation dinner, sitting on the top table with just half a dozen people, including Princess Alexandra and Rupert Murdoch, between us!) The day after Maxwell's phone call, the bid was formally announced: 500p cash with an alternative offer in the form of a security convertible into BPCC shares.

During the first bid we had been careful not to indulge in any mud-slinging. All of the Sunday newspapers were on Maxwell's side and some of the other newspapers tended to favour him. And we could not afford to alienate our solidly supportive institutional shareholders who had no taste for unsavoury verbal battles. October 1984 was different. We had already beaten Maxwell. He had just acquired the *Daily Mirror*, thus losing some press support. We felt that we should wage a robust campaign, especially as the price offered was high. In the preceding months Price Waterhouse, on our behalf, had carefully analysed the available accounts of all Maxwell's companies and assessed the financial effects of all public announcements. They produced a combined, adjusted debt/equity statement. Kleinworts also initiated a study into the ownership of the Maxwell empire. The trail led to New York where the Pergamon Holdings Foundation appeared to be owned 100% by a Raymond de Geoffrey de la Pradelle in Paris, who in turn reported to Liechtenstein. By coincidence, de la Pradelle's office was next door to that of our main French associate, Michel Habourdin, and with his help we mounted an enquiry which sadly yielded nothing. I had the headlines in mind already; 'Maxwell's mystery man', or 'The French Connection!'

Public relations were of great importance. We decided to move to a new company and chose Anthony Cardew and Josceline Grove because they said that they could probably swing the Sunday papers our way. In the event they succeeded with *The Observer*, neutralised *The Sunday Times* and left only *The Sunday Telegraph* firmly on Maxwell's side. In other ways too, the part played by Cardew and Grove was immensely helpful.

An essential part of our defence was to get people interested in Maxwell's financial fragility and the mystery of the ultimate ownership. Neither task was particularly easy at that time. I remember calling on Jeff Benson, the vice-chairman of NatWest, and showing him the results of our investigation into the finances of the Maxwell empire. I pointed out that Maxwell had a number of shareholdings in Fleet, Reuters, Rediffusion and Empire Stores and that normal banking practice was to lend only 50% on securities whereas Maxwell was being lent nearly 100%. I said that Maxwell would not be able to do with Waddingtons what he had done with BPCC and I explained why. I emphasised how customers and senior employees would be disaffected. Finally I suggested that it seemed that when the deals were big enough and the players persuasive enough, the normal checks and safety precautions of the banks were often forgotten.

We put the following message over to financial journalists on a personal basis: 'The delay in the arrival of the BPCC offer document to Waddingtons shareholders raises several questions. Has Maxwell over-reached himself? Was the bid premature and unplanned? Is Mr Maxwell having difficulty with the necessary financial backing? The cash drain on BPCC has been significant in spite of the injection of the £45 million from the liquidation of Bishopsgate. Furthermore, another survival plan is currently being pressed on the BPCC Watford workforce with inevitable redundancies (471 were quoted on 26 October in the *Watford Observer*) and the consequent high cost and increased borrowings. Mr Maxwell's bankers may at last be getting cold feet as they are asked for even more money to acquire Waddingtons.'

It is worth recalling that Robert Maxwell was well thought of by many people in 1984. In November the Financial Times reported on a Taylor Nelson survey of UK chief executives and managing directors who had been asked who they admired most for their overall excellence. Maxwell came third – just ahead of Ian McGregor, the well known head of British Steel. Also, it was not easy to interest the press in our concern about the ownership of Maxwell's empire or his stretched finances. Lord Rothermere let his ace reporter John Rawlings loose on it however, and he was the first to highlight what became a matter of great concern much later on. But this was after the posting of Maxwell's offer document on 22 November. The document contained two big surprises. The share alternative had been dropped, leaving only the cash offer. In addition to this, a final date of 13 December was named, which left the Maxwell camp no room for manoeuvre because we could wait until the day for increasing the bid had passed before announcing our half year results and profit forecast. We discussed the merits of Maxwell's tactics. He had restricted his actions, but at the same time Christmas was looming up and most people would want to get the bid over and done with. It was also typical of Maxwell's hustling tactics. He often made an offer and fixed a deadline. Of course, he was lucky to get away with the dropping of the share offer. *The Times* reported that Peter Fraser of the City Takeover Panel said, 'This is a rather unsatisfactory and tiresome outcome, but since they did not commit themselves to a value for the convertible offer, the withdrawal seems legitimate.' The Panel had been told that a 'change in market conditions made the intended alternative proposal unattractive.' In actual fact the BPCC share price had only dropped from 178p to 173p!

500p was however a high bid. The Maxwell camp made the point that the Waddingtons share price had been 104p before the bids of 1983 and they forecast Waddingtons profits at £5.5 million (a cunning tactic intended to put us on the spot). The offer document went on to say, 'It is possible that your directors will attempt to distract you from the merits of our offers with adverse comments on the BPCC-Pergamon Group. The fact is that the record of BPCC with the Pergamon Group of companies speaks for itself and that, in any case, in the context of very attractive cash offers, such comments are irrelevant.' The relevance or otherwise was the subject of some discussion. A *Guardian* reporter wrote, 'If you sell a dog you make sure that it has a good home and that the buyers are capable of caring for it. Surely the employees of a public company are entitled to the same consideration.'

29 November was the last day on which Maxwell could increase his offer. It seemed unlikely that an increase would come but Maxwell was unpredictable. We had our ripostes ready just in case. The City journalists wrote the story and put the papers to bed. But we were not so sure. It would have been possible to post the document just before midnight in order to get everybody on the wrong foot next morning. But no increase came. We then posted our rejection document on 4 December with our half year profit. We delayed our profit forecast for the full year until 10 December and were able to top Maxwell's high estimate. As usual, our defence rested on performance and the credibility of our forecasts rather than any verbal infighting. There was also the question of the Warburgs shareholding. (See Appendix G.)

Warburgs had started to build up their stake during the first bid. We made the usual visit to them but got short shrift. They made it clear to us that they had no concern for anything but the financial performance of their funds. During 1984 one of their fund managers told us that he confidently expected a bid and was preparing his holding in order to benefit from it. By the time of the bid in October, the holding was substantial and therefore crucial. The stake included some of Sainsbury's pension fund money. Maxwell wanted Sainsbury's to instruct Warburgs to accept the bid and told Sainsbury's that they could have his Watford site in return. Sainsbury's objected to Maxwell's pressurising and told Warburgs that they could dispose of the Waddingtons shares. Working for us we had the extremely competent and level-headed Christopher Eugster of Kleinworts and the highly regarded Julian Cazalet of Cazenoves. Warburgs were not prepared to support us so, at the last minute, Kleinworts bought the holding and it was subsequently placed by Cazenoves with various investors.

The famous campaign about the ownership of Maxwell's empire did not get going until very late, in spite of our efforts. John Rawlings started it with a powerful piece in *The Mail on Sunday* on 2 December. But on the same day *The Sunday Telegraph* referred to the 'indomitable Robert Maxwell', and ended the piece, 'We still believe the Waddingtons shareholders should accept.'

The breakthrough came when the *Financial Times* sent Duncan Campbell-Smith to Vaduz, the capital of Liechtenstein, on 3 December. He produced a half page article for the Saturday, 8 December paper, which was devastating to the Maxwell camp. He quoted Maxwell as saying that he was not the owner of the *Daily Mirror* and had never said so. My wife said, 'I'm sure he did say so.' I got the newspaper cuttings out immediately and started to phone the City journalists to refer them to the front page of *The Times* of 14 July, when Maxwell had said, 'I am the new proprietor 100%. And I want that to be understood very clearly. There can only be one boss and that is me.' We scored with *The Sunday Times* and *The Observer*.

On 12 December, Ansbacher, the merchant bank representing Maxwell, issued a press release, which said that they could not win. People started to phone us with congratulations, but we were not taken in at all. They wanted the price to drop so that they could nip in and buy shares. I thought that the Takeover Panel should declare the contest over. It was like conceding a putt at golf and, when your opponent carelessly misses it, claiming the hole.

But by 3.30pm on 13 December we really had won, and for us the relief was enormous. For Maxwell, on the other hand, the deluge was just beginning. The publicity campaign we had waged had only just got going. For the next few weeks the press coverage of the Liechtenstein connection was overwhelming. Maxwell did recover his reputation with some people because he was permitted to go on an even bigger spending binge later on. But the number of people like Cazenoves and M and G who refused to deal with him increased greatly as a consequence of the bid.

Postscript: Before the year was out, Maxwell had disposed of almost his entire shareholding in Waddingtons, which yielded a substantial profit. This puffed up the dismal BPCC figures for the year ending December 1984. I could not help wondering if the rascal had planned to lose in order to sell out at a high price!

CHAPTER THIRTEEN

THE MAXWELL BIDS – THE LIGHTER SIDE

So far as the press are concerned it is a good idea to have a few snappy answers ready. If they are suitably pungent, satirical and funny, so much the better. Richard Hanwell, Norton Opax's opportunistic chief executive, described himself at the time of his bid for Waddingtons as a devout Christian, as if that made his greedy attack more like a sacred duty. A reporter asked me about this. 'What do you think? He says he's a Christian.' I replied, 'So was the Grand Inquisitor.'

Robert Maxwell made an even better target. He acquired his famous nickname, 'The Bouncing Czech', when he became the MP for Buckingham. It was a nickname he hated. He much preferred to be disliked than to be laughed at. That made him more vulnerable. So I spent time conjuring up remarks which the press would like. My favourite came up when Maxwell announced that, on acquiring Waddingtons, he would make me his second in command. I said, 'I don't want to play second fiddle to a one man band.'

Other quips I had which were used on suitable occasions (and not all occasions are suitable!) were:

'Yes, I met him once; my luck had to run out eventually.'

'I decided to take an instant dislike to him; it saves so much time.'

'I'll never forget him no matter how hard I try.'

When we produced the famous 46.2%, the body of shareholders who allowed us to state that they had agreed not to accept the bid, Maxwell said in a TV interview, 'Victor Watson has thrown a googly at me.' In reply, to

TV and the press I said, 'That reminded me of the spy thrillers by writers like John Buchan. The spy who speaks impeccable English gives himself away by saying "thrown a googly", when any freeborn Englishman knows it's "bowls a googly".'

The *Daily Mirror* staff had a field day when Maxwell took over. At the time of his well-publicised efforts to send food to Ethiopia he was nicknamed Citizen Grain. When his helicopter landed on the roof they said, 'The ego has landed.'

They told the story that his aides had planned a state funeral in case the gallant captain snuffed it. When Maxwell found out he was furious. 'Far too expensive,' he said, 'and in any case I don't expect to be away for more than three days.'

I suppose I might have had a writ when I spoke at a Web Offset Conference with Maxwell employees present. I declared, 'Mr Maxwell is Europe's largest printer, so large in fact that it might be possible to print a short history of Czechoslovakia on the seat of his trousers.'

But to Maxwell it all added up to making his presence felt. And he did have astonishing presence. When he came into a room you sensed it at once. Giles Brandreth told me that at one of the famous Maxwell birthday parties at his offices at Headington Hall, it seemed that wherever you were in the house or the marquee you could hear Maxwell. Then Giles discovered that Maxwell had a microphone attached to his lapel, which picked up his voice and relayed it to speakers all over the place. Yes, Maxwell wanted to be noticed. Like the saying of the Duc de Rochefoucauld – 'Love me if you will, hate me if you must, but don't ignore me.' Taunts and gags he would haughtily ignore. But we found that it enlivened our meetings to think up a few new lines like:

'He's lost his way and the same thing seems to be happening to his marbles.'

'He is an express train with a wheel off.'

'His membership of the Labour Party is a flag of convenience.'

David Perry came out with the best, which appeared in the press: 'He's a misguided missile.'

In the early days of the 1983 bid, my brother John and I met Donald Davies, a well-known executive in the printing trade. He told us that he had been offered a job by Maxwell, as managing director elect of BPCC. On the day that he was to start he arrived at Maxwell House, Worship Street and was in the waiting room ready to be called by Maxwell. Another BPCC executive, walking by, saw Donald and said, 'Hello Donald, what are you doing here?'

'I'm starting work here today as the new managing director elect', replied Donald.

'Well,' said the other, 'after work let's meet here and I'll take you to the pub across the road and introduce you to all the other managing directors elect!'

In the later stages of the 1984 bid, Maxwell declared that when he won, Victor Watson would be sacked and David Perry would be offered a job. A printing trade magazine published pictures of David and myself. Under a picture of a smiling Victor was the caption 'Sacked'. Under a picture of a frowning David was the caption 'Can Stay'.

CHAPTER FOURTEEN

WHAT BECAME OF WADDINGTONS?

I AM OFTEN asked, 'What became of Waddingtons?' I reply that parts were sold and the printing interests were amalgamated with those of Bowaters (renamed Rexam), and the combined business was renamed Communisis, which is now one of the UK's largest printers, serving mainly the financial markets. But if I look back to 1983, Waddingtons comprised games and playing cards, a strong position in packaging with folding cartons, labels and plastic containers for food and beverages and, in addition, printing enterprises including continuous stationery and postage stamps, to name but two of a number of product areas. Of this impressive list only a remnant of the printing activities survive. None of the buildings of 1983 are part of the new business. Only a handful of the people are still involved. The old company is no more.

But in January of 1985 we were riding high. We had defeated Robert Maxwell conclusively. We had battered his reputation and we had enhanced our own. We had a lively management team led by David Perry. I had tried to get David to join us some years previously but he had declined. However, when Robert Maxwell acquired the British Printing Corporation, David, one of his senior managers, was more easily persuaded in 1981 to come to Waddingtons. He very soon became the managing director and, with the help of another stalwart director, Ken Lunn, revived a business which had been through a sticky patch. David is a born leader, as one would expect in a man who captained the English rugby team. He knew the trade, was approachable and liked by the customers and shareholders, listened and had great energy. When the bid arrived in 1983, I led the defence and David ran the business. Of course the jobs overlapped as I knew so many people connected with the company and David knew the customers and shareholders too. We worked as a partnership and it was effective. I stood for continuity and commitment. He stood for change.

During 1984 we appointed a new non-executive director, Michael Abrahams, a Yorkshire businessman and the deputy chairman of the Prudential Assurance Company. We also had to face the inevitable retirement of Norman Gaunt, our brilliant chemist who became a director. He had developed new features of folding cartons and quality control systems, and he could even be said to have invented our plastics business, which started with one machine to produce deep drawn thermoformed containers for Schweppes and led to the supply of containers for Van Den Berghs and many other well known food companies.

In the January of 1985 we already had a plan to grow Waddingtons organically through investment in the latest technology and also by acquisition of complementary businesses. During 1984 we had acquired Vickers Business Forms with a rights issue at the same time. We had also taken over the House of Questa, one of the few printers of postage stamps in the UK. The Post Office, a major customer, had declared that they intended to have just two suppliers of lithographed stamps instead of three, and we concluded that we would be the one for the chop because we could take such a blow on the chin whereas either of the other two suppliers might have had to close down. So, we approached House of Questa (who incidentally feared that we would be the chosen supplier) and soon agreed a purchase of their business which would leave the incumbent management in charge.

In 1986 we bought Comet Products in Chelmsford, Massachusetts, an excellent injection moulder of plastic drinking cups. This was the inspired initiative of Philip Brain who ran our plastic packaging business. Phil also engaged Clem Izzi to manage Comet, a task he performed with distinction. The idea was to apply our thermoforming technology to Comet, but it never worked well because of the different know-how required. This led, in a few years, to our purchase of Hopple Plastics in Cincinnati so that our products could be made there. Meanwhile Comet proved to be a very good investment. In the next few years three other US plastics businesses were acquired; they were California Cutlery, Carthage Cup and Cups Illustrated. This gave us a nationwide coverage in the plastic cups and cutlery business. Our successors sold the US business in food services (cups, cutlery, etc.) in 2000, and it is now run by Mike Evans who started from university in Waddingtons' personnel department and went to the US for us for a stint of a year or two and stayed. Called WNA (short for Waddingtons North America), the company is very successful.

In March of 1987 we acquired Gilmour and Dean, a Glasgow printer which owned Chorley and Pickersgill, the highly successful web offset printers in Leeds, specialising in printing for the financial markets. Chorleys was a great asset to us and Michael Mitchell, who started as an estimator and became the managing director of the company, was eventually made a director of Waddingtons. The operation is still one of the jewels in the crown of Communisis. Michael Mitchell retired a few years ago. In June of 1987 we bought the UK star of the pharmaceutical packaging field, Johnsen and Jorgensen. I had spent much time getting to know John Jorgensen, who finally told me that it would suit the families to sell the business. It was sad for a fine company of over a hundred years, but a sell-out is often inevitable as families diverge and have different views and priorities. The packaging industry considered it to be a coup for us, but in truth we had a year or two of difficulties with the business.

In 1989 my younger brother John left the company. In the same year my brother Beric (three years younger than me) died in the process of a heart transplant operation. He ran the games business very well, and was a great salesman and a lovable character. So by 1993 when I retired at sixty-five, it was the end of the Watson connection. I think it is fair to say that it was also the end of our personal ethos. I wrote a preamble to our business plan of the time. It went as follows:

Selling Things Off

This idea is bound to crop up during the discussions. It should be considered against the background of the company's ethos. We are not simply a money-making machine. We are a group of people, drawn together in a most interesting and stimulating enterprise. The dividends and the growth in share value are like a licence fee to the owners so that we be allowed to continue with our absorbing work. The financial results are a measure of our success. We all want to be better off of course, but we are not in it just for the money. The achievement, the contribution to society and the self-satisfaction are important aspects. If we start to think of our various businesses as chattels, as mere money producing machines, then we shall begin to destroy our ethos. Yes, we need to consider the future viability of each part of our company and we need to redirect our resources. Occasionally it may make sense to sell a part. If we do it, then it should be because it is really necessary and we should all feel a sense of loss at the parting with good friends and colleagues. There is a notion that emotion and loyalty in business are things of the past. I believe that to be a passing fashion. Furthermore I believe that the companies with heart and soul will triumph over those which are mere money machines.

I had been a prime mover in the sale of our greetings card business, Valentines of Dundee. And I had tested the water in regard to a sale of our games business, but only to see if a very high price could be achieved, so high that it would have seemed foolish not to accept. I did not want to sell the games business but I could see the business sense of it at the right price. But emotionally I shrank from sales of companies which I felt betrayed our people. On my retirement there must have been a feeling that an obstacle to disposals had been removed. Our knowledgeable, competent and dedicated company secretary, Peter Stephens, had already retired, and his connection was even older than mine as his uncle was involved in Waddingtons before my grandfather. Yes, Waddingtons without us had a different ethos without trying. David Perry followed me as chairman. The chief executive was Martin Buckley, an accountant by profession, who had worked at Linpac in the UK and the USA. He was competent, analytical and systematic; a good partner for David who had the people skills and knew customers, shareholders and employees and was liked. Our finance director was Geoff Gibson, ex-Price Waterhouse, a very open and pragmatic man (he paid his way through articles as a Rugby League professional). He had the confidence of his colleagues and all the accountants in the company and could tell which ones were pessimistic and which were optimistic; yes, there are optimistic accountants. Geoff joined us from Price Waterhouse in 1985 and became finance director in 1987 when Chris Bowes, our shrewd finance director, had heart trouble and had to retire altogether. It was fortunate that we had permanent ill-health insurance in place. It was an idea I had in 1984 when thinking of what Maxwell might do if he gained control of Waddingtons. One possibility was that he would make life so intolerable that an executive might have a heart attack. So we got permanent ill-health insurance in place, never thinking that a comparatively young and energetic man like Chris would be an early casualty. Another safeguard I instituted (against the wishes of lawyers and pensions advisers) was the appointment of three permanent pension trustees, one being Noble Lowndes and the other two Peter Stephens and me. I figured that if Maxwell won, he would appoint his own nominees and then use the pension fund for his risky schemes. (It did happen later with BPCC.) The three permanent trustees could only be removed by application to the Courts and I reckoned that Maxwell would not want the adverse publicity of such a case and might lose anyway, although in 1984 Maxwell still had many supporters and believers. The two non-executive directors were Michael Abrahams and, from 1990, David Sykes, the senior partner of Hepworth and Chadwick, which became Eversheds later on. The company secretary was Martin Young, who joined us when we bought Gilmour and Dean and became company secretary in 1990. He was a very safe 'pair of hands', as is vitally important for a complex company like Waddingtons.

On 30 November 1994, Waddingtons announced the sale of Waddingtons Games to Hasbro for £50 million. Just prior to this the company had bought IMCA Beheer BV, a large Dutch folding carton maker, for £44.9 million (financed by a rights issue), which reinforced the company's position in folding cartons. The company's own folding carton division had moved to a brand new, purpose built factory in Leeds in 1991, causing the sale and demolition of the famous factory in Wakefield Road and the building of a separate head office across the road. The new factory had space for expansion, and, with the addition of IMCA, this placed Waddingtons in the top flight of carton makers in Europe and made it clear that this was the way forward for the company. As for games, I had been asked in July 1994 by Torquil Norman of Bluebird Toys if Waddingtons Games might be sold to them. He said they had £20 million in cash. I told David Perry, who confided in me that Hasbro had approached the company about the sale of games and that they had just said that with sales of £25 million and profit of £4 million, the price would have to be very high, certainly over £40 million – too high for Bluebird.

The announcement of the sale for £50 million of a company with sales of £25.92 million and operating profit of £3.45 million sparked a flurry of press comment and many calls and letters for me. A typical example was the headline in the *Financial Times*; 'Waddington passes Monopoly to Hasbro and collects £50 million'. When the media asked me for my thoughts, I said that I was sad that the long association was at an end but that I could not fault the business logic. I explained that the two very largest toy companies, Mattel and Hasbro, were eager to acquire brands and the fact that two bidders were there increased the price. 'The price is high', I stated. Furthermore, I said that the toys and games industry had become increasingly international and as Waddingtons did not own Monopoly and had only Cluedo, as a truly international brand its position was weak. Oddly enough Waddingtons did not mention the latter point in its rationale, but said simply that the plan was to major on packaging and specialist printing where higher returns were available. Waddingtons Games Ltd doubled its profit in the first year of Hasbro's ownership. Since then I know from a reliable but unofficial source that the sales of Monopoly have doubled in the UK and Cluedo (Clue in the USA) is selling well too. Even more surprising is the news that a Waddingtons product, Top Trumps, has sold fifteen million units in the last five years. So, with the benefit of hindsight, I was wrong to say that £50 million was a high price. For Hasbro it was a bargain. At the time though, £50 million did seem to be a high price and there was considerable support for the sale of the company, especially in the City. But many were astonished that Waddingtons would part with games, playing cards and jigsaw puzzles for which the company was so well known. A competitor put it in a nutshell to me; 'Now you'll be just a boring old packaging company like the rest of us.' Martin Buckley was quoted in the press as saying that packaging and printing offered better margins! It was a dangerous forecast as events have proved. Since then, packaging and printing have been hammered on price because of increased productivity and demand which has not kept pace. The Waddingtons Games employees felt badly let down and expected (correctly as events proved) that the Leeds factory would be closed. All other Waddingtons employees knew that everything could be for sale. Astonishingly, the Vickers Business Forms (renamed Waddington Business Forms) had been sold in 1993, the Gilmour and Dean business in Glasgow had been sold, (but not Chorley and Pickersgill), Plastona was sold in 1996 and in 1998, just four years after the purchase of IMCA and the sale of games, Waddingtons Cartons and IMCA were sold to Low and Bonar for £67 million and are now owned by Nampak, the South African company. Most of this came after the sudden retirement of David Perry in 1997. He had heart trouble and told me that he found the executive life too much. It left Martin Buckley with a non-executive chairman in Michael Orr who did not know the company and could not be a partner to Martin in any way, except dealing with the City, and the shareholders. It was bad for the company that there was no rapport between Martin Buckley and his chairman. Not only did Martin lose his senior partner, David Perry, but business became more difficult in all departments. At the time, I believe that Martin was convinced that the City did not understand the problems, so he and Geoff Gibson came to the feeling that they should try to engineer a management buyout. The April 1999 accounts showed sales of £257.2 million and profit before tax of £23.3 million (well down on 1998). The sales were divided between pharmaceutical packaging at £59.9 million, food services (USA) at £93.3 million and printing at £105 million. Michael Orr, the chairman, stood down at the AGM in July 1999 and was replaced by John Hollowood. The management buyout was announced in September at a price of £300 million. The shares at the time were 237p, valuing the company at £251.5 million. The City and analysts said 'Too low; £320 million nearer the mark!'

A consequence of the proposed management buyout was that it put the company 'in play' as they say in financial circles; 'open to offers', in other words. Sure enough, on 26 October 1999 a relatively obscure company called John Mansfield announced its bid. John Mansfield Group Ltd was ostensibly a timber merchant. In reality it was the acquisition vehicle of Active Value Fund Managers Ltd, owned largely by Brian Myerson and Julian Treger, who were corporate investors. Their acquisition team in the case of Waddingtons was Stuart Wallis and David Jones, both experienced in packaging and printing. The bid could have been described as cheeky and opportunistic, and it was an indictment of Waddingtons at the time that no such comments were made. Unprofitable Mansfield with a market worth of £17.5 million and sales of £12 million per annum was bidding to acquire Waddingtons at a price of £318 million. The business of Mansfield with such a catch would be mostly composed of Waddingtons, and that was the object of the exercise.

Wallis, the prime mover, had held senior positions with Rexam plc (formerly Bowater plc), including those of chief executive officer at Bowater Europe and chief executive of Bowater Print and Packaging. He had also been the chief executive of Fisons. David Jones had been chief executive of Rexam's Octagon and Containers Divisions and finance director of Bowater Europe. With the management buyout on the table the Waddingtons board were obliged to be divided. The non-executive directors Messrs Hollowood, Abrahams and Sykes had to see to the interests and rights of the shareholders, while Messrs Buckley and Gibson were after the management buyout. Waddingtons were not in a good position to repel the bid from Mansfield. Ros Snowden, the *Yorkshire Post* deputy City editor, put it well on 26 October 1999:

> Packaging group Waddington had both good and bad news for shareholders yesterday. The good is that it is in talks with new bidders which should hike up the price of the company and the bad is that it has discovered a stock shortfall at one of its US subsidiaries.
>
> The Leeds-based company said further approaches have been made to the company since news of last month's talks with NatWest Equity Partners.

It is understood that two other private equity firms have joined the race to take Waddington private and the likeliest candidates are Phildrew Ventures and Schroder Ventures.

If either of these two are successful they will back the management takeover led by chief executive Martin Buckley and finance director Geoffrey Gibson.

But late yesterday another bidder, timber products maker John Mansfield, confirmed it was in talks with Waddington.

John Mansfield, now a shell company controlled by Brian Myerson and Julian Treger, launched a bid for building products group Marley in December, but was outbid by Belgian rival Etax.

Waddington said that discussions were ongoing and the Board does not anticipate being able to announce any offer in the near future.

There has been speculation that a bidding war could break out for the company and a price tag of between 325p and 350p a share has been talked about.

But yesterday the shares closed the day down 4.5%, a fall of 11.5p to 245p, following the news of stock irregularities at Lermer, a subsidiary of Waddingtons' US pharmaceutical packaging business.

The stock shortfall at the US plastic bottle-making subsidiary is under investigation and is expected to lead to a £2.5 million charge to be taken in the first half results. It is understood that the shortfall is a one-off and is unlikely to impact on the rest of the group, but the news was not well received by the market and is thought to have brought the price tag back down to nearer 300p.

Following the stock shortfall the group is investigating whether there has been any foul play at the US site, but it is too early to tell.

Aside from this, the group said overall trading for the six months to September 1999 had been in line with expectations.

This follows a difficult year for the group when a slowdown in trading during last October, November and December led to a profits warning in February.

Pre-tax profits for the year to April came in at £23.3 million, down from £39.6 million, on the back of sales of £295.1 million.

The group had been hit by oversupply in the UK, customer and technical problems in the US and the loss of a big US customer.

In June the group reported an improvement in sales following a return in confidence among its key pharmaceutical customers.

A month later outgoing chairman Michael Orr told the annual general meeting that underlying sales in May, June and July were 'satisfactorily ahead of those for the comparative period last year'.

There was much for the non-executive directors of Waddingtons to do – deal with possible offers; discuss matters with bankers and lawyers who would have had to advise on the law and the Stock Exchange rules governing such situations; discuss what to do if all the bids and possible bids failed. It was a torrid time for them. Meanwhile, Messrs Wallis and Jones had a plan. It was hinted at by Terry Ulrick in his *Printing World* article of 11 December 1999 as follows:

> Waddington, the £250 million packaging group name still associated with Monopoly, hopes to pass Go with one of the bids lurking at its front door. Up front, eager to go and agreed by Waddington itself, is last week's bid by the John Mansfield Group offering £318.7 million for the Leeds company. However, analysts believe the Mansfield approach will be the catalyst that sparks off further interest which could culminate in a battle for dominance of the UK packaging sector.
>
> Waddington, which sold its famous games interest to Hasbro five years ago, has been beset by problems of late. Three profit warnings, an admitted shortfall in sales and irregularities at a US subsidiary, have all added to an uncomfortable year for chief executive Martin Buckley.
>
> All this despite a substantially increased presence in direct mail, including the £12 million acquisition of the Howitt Group family business.
>
> The John Mansfield Group is regarded as an acquisition vehicle headed by Stuart Wallis and David Jones and backed by international corporate investors Julian Treger and Brian Myerson. Messrs Wallis and Jones are veterans of the packaging scene – Mr Wallis was a former chief executive of Bowater's printing and packaging operations and Mr Jones headed Bowater Containers. John Mansfield's name was in the British financial press in 1998 when it raised bids, later aborted, for Marley and for Norcros.
>
> The fact that Bowater is now Rexam and the packaging market leader, and that it has top packaging experience at the helm has sparked speculation that Mansfield may have bigger ambitions to eventually dominate the sector. The Mansfield bid, which the independent Waddington directors have accepted so far, is 28.6 new Mansfield shares and £1 in cash for each Waddington share. This values each Waddington share at 300p and places the overall value at £318.7 million.
>
> Major Waddington shareholders Phillips and Drew Fund Management, Aberforth Partners and Aberforth Unit Trust, which together account for 19.1% of Waddington, have given their irrevocable acceptance to the deal. However, Waddington assumes that the Mansfield bid will flush out

alternative offers. An MBO team led by Mr Buckley is believed to be seeking financial backing for a bid that will hit the table shortly. Another bid, probably from the US, is also thought to be on the cards.

The Mansfield bid represents a premium of more than 48% above the Waddington closing price of 202p on September 17, the day the company revealed it had received a preliminary approach. Waddington shareholders on the register at the close of business on December 10 will receive the interim dividend of 5.25p per share announced on November 24. These interim results showed Waddington revealing a £2.2 million dip in profits compared with the same period in the previous year.

Soon after the successful acquisition of Waddingtons, Mansfield's plan to buy Rexam's printing division for £85 million was revealed in April 2000. The division had been built up by acquisition and included the likes of McCorquodales and Standard Cheque. So it was a fine stable of printing businesses in the new company, which was renamed Communisis plc. The last annual report of Mansfields (April 2000) hardly mentioned the timber business which had made a loss in the year under review. But the final paragraph of the chief executive's report revealed the strategy:

The strategy to deliver increased shareholder value

We have previously indicated that Mansfield's strategy is to acquire underperforming public companies and realise shareholder value by implementing strategic and cultural management changes to improve performance. This can be achieved by intensive and focused operational management of core business to maximise sales growth, margins and cash generation, reinforced by the sale of businesses that are too small, too slow to turn around or peripheral to the core focus. The acquisitions of Waddington plc and the printing division of Rexam plc exactly fit this overall strategy.

D.E.A. Jones
Chief Executive.

By the end of 2000 the US businesses had been sold, as had all the UK packaging interests except the label printing business in Gateshead. (The latter survived until 2004 when it was closed, presumably because it could not be sold. It was the last of the old Waddingtons). The old board of directors went with no ceremony. Martin Buckley lost his job as David Jones moved in pronto. Geoff Gibson stayed for a while to help with disposals. The new chief set about running the cleverly assembled assortment of printing companies, almost all of which fitted the aim of having more to them than just putting ink on to paper. Martin Young continued as company secretary. He could write a much more interesting account than I can, but I have not asked him for information in order not to put him in a difficult position. In any case he is still involved with the Communisis pension scheme on which many of us rely. The offer document for Waddingtons pledged that our pension rights would be safeguarded.

In the seven years since the takeover, the company has not been successful. Sales of about £250–£300 million have been maintained. Two years have shown losses, in particular 2004 and 2006. The 2006 annual report uses the words 'demanding' and 'challenging', and those of us in business see at once that they mean 'unprofitable'. In October 2006 it was announced that David Jones had 'stood down' and soon after that Denise Moran, the sales chief, also left. When the market place becomes crowded and all around are companies endeavouring to be different and at the same time more productive, it is difficult to succeed. It is possible to make too many changes out of desperation. The March '06 newsletter of Communisis quoted David Jones saying of the Altrincham business, 'As ever the site is impressive.' Later that year it was closed and moved to Leeds. The new chief executive refers to mistakes in that decision without actually blaming anybody. In fact the new man, Steve Vaughan, gives the impression of really knowing what to do and how to carry everyone along with him. We all wish him success. As I said earlier, the former Waddingtons is no more, and yet I feel a loyalty to the mutation of the old warrior. In bygone days we said that we used printing as a means to an end and not an end in itself. We never thought of ourselves as purely printers. That is once again the message of Steve Vaughan, but now it is against the background of a world of electronic communication, an opportunity which would excite my grandfather even more than photographic colour separation and the marvels of 100 years ago.

APPENDICES

APPENDIX A

(RELATES TO CHAPTERS TWO AND THREE)

JOHN WADDINGTON LTD

Minutes of a meeting of directors held at the registered office of the company, Gt Wilson Street, Leeds, on Thursday, 6 March 1913.

<u>Present:</u>   Mr Edgar Lupton   (Chairman)
            Mr R. B. Stephens
            Mr Waddington

The minutes of the previous meeting were read and confirmed.

The chairman informed Mr Waddington that there were several matters of importance which he was desirous of investigating and upon which it would be necessary to question him, and in view of this Mr Arthur Willey, solicitor, had been invited to attend the meeting. With Mr Waddington's concurrence Mr Willey was accordingly invited into the room.

Mr Lupton told Mr Waddington that the directors had found he had received at least two sums of money for respectively £50 and £25 from two employees of the company, that no mention of the receipt of this sum had been made by him to the directors, that the consent of the directors should have been obtained in connection therewith, and the moneys handed over to the company who were entitled to them.

Mr Waddington admitted that he had received the two sums of money mentioned and that he had not informed the directors of his having done so. He also expressed his regret that he had acted in this manner, stating further that he was prepared to hand the amounts back at the rate of £1 per week or upon further consideration he thought he could mortgage certain life policies to provide the money at once.

Questioned as to what explanation he could give regarding certain entries in the books of the company under the name of Young and another man named Ward who were each put down as having received £1.15s.0d. per week whereas in fact Young had only received 10/- per week. Mr Waddington acknowledged that Young had only been paid 10/- per week and that the balance had been received by himself but it had been expended upon the company's behalf in defraying his own expenses. He further stated that the facts were the same with regard to the entries made under the name of Ward, but did not attempt to justify the irregularities.

At the request of the directors Mr Waddington retired from the room and Miss Laing, the secretary was called in. She informed the Board that at Mr Waddington's request she had entered Young's wage as £1.15s.0d. per week although she was aware that Young only received 10/- of the amount. She expressed her dissatisfaction with many of the entries in the artists salary and payment book, where a number of payments were entered although there was nothing to show what they were for. She further stated that without receiving any particulars as to what they were for Mr Waddington had been in the habit of getting cash from her out of the petty cash for expenses he stated he had incurred. Miss Laing retired and Mr Dixon was then called in and he stated that he was aware that Mr Waddington was taking the balance of Mr Young's wages for himself and that Mr Waddington had acknowledged to him that Ward was a mythical person and was not employed by the company, also that Mr Waddington was putting the money entered against Ward's name into his own pocket.

After Mr Dixon had retired Mr Watson was sent for. He stated that he was by no means satisfied with the result of the year's trading but was not in a position to put his hands upon any leakages.

After these interviews Mr Waddington again joined the directors who asked him if he had any justification for these irregularities which he admitted. Mr Waddington had nothing further to say and was then informed by the chairman that the directors took an extremely serious view of the matter, whereupon Mr Waddington offered to forthwith tender his resignation as managing director of the company. He then wrote out such resignation and handed same to the chairman with the request that he at least might be allowed to stay until the following day.

This request the directors considered and granted to Mr Waddington, they further resolved to call a meeting of the directors for the following morning at ten o'clock at the offices of Messrs Bond, Barwick and Peake.

Edgar Lupton

JOHN WADDINGTON LTD

Minutes of a meeting of the directors held at the offices of Messrs Bond, Barwick and Peake in Basinghall Street, Leeds on Friday, 7 March 1913.

<u>Present:</u> Mr Edgar Lupton   (Chairman)
Mr A. C. Peake
Mr R. B. Stephens
Mr Arthur Willey also attended

The minutes of the previous meeting were read, approved and signed.

Mr Waddington's letter of resignation was submitted to the Board who accepted same and passed a resolution in the form of the following letter which was handed by them to Mr Waddington:

Gt Wilson Street
Leeds
7 March 1913

Dear Sir

The directors have considered your resignation at a meeting this morning, and decided to accept the same at once. In view of your earnest solicitation last night that you should have some consideration at our hands, we have decided, that although your services terminate today you shall be paid your salary for a further two weeks but it must be distinctly understood that you must not go to the works; on the other hand we have no doubt in case of necessity you will be glad to furnish us with any assistance or information in regard to the business during that period. In regard to the admitted receipt by you of the sum of £75 by way of premiums from servants in our employment, you have no right whatever to retain these moneys, and although we strongly deprecate your conduct in regard to the matter, under the circumstances now within our knowledge, we do not propose to insist upon repayment.

> Yours truly
> (signed)   *Edgar Lupton*   )   Directors
> "   *A. Copson Peake*   )   of
> "   *R. B. Stephens*   )   John Waddington Ltd

Upon recording same, Mr Waddington expressed his readiness to assist the company in any way which might be required of him by the directors, but asked them to let him have a month's salary so that he might be able to look round for some means of livelihood. He also asked that the railway pass paid for by the company might be allowed to remain in his possession for the same purpose until it expired.

The directors after considering the matter passed the following resolution which took the form of a letter to Mr Waddington:

7 March

Dear Sir

Following our letter of this morning and with reference to our subsequent conversation with you we confirm that we are agreeable to pay you two full weeks' salary from this date and providing nothing on your part shall in the view of the directors be prejudicial of this expiration of that time. We also confirm that it is understood you are to have the privilege of retaining the company's pass for one month from this date. We would repeat that you must not go to the offices or works except at the request of the directors.

> Yours faithfully
> Edgar Lupton
> Chairman of Directors

The directors then interviewed Mr Watson who was appointed as manager (with salary to be arranged) and Mr Dixon who was appointed secretary and cashier in place of Miss Laing.

Edgar Lupton

APPENDIX B

(APPENDICES B–E ARE RELEVANT TO DOUGLAS BREARLEY'S STORY, AND HAVE BEEN GATHERED OR WRITTEN BY VICTOR WATSON JNR.)

Waddingtons guaranteed Mr Vauvelle's company twenty pounds worth of work per week in exchange for preference and priority. A piece about Achille Vauvelle appeared in the Waddingtons' *Team Magazine* **as follows:**

I found Mr Achille Vauvelle in his studio, entrenched behind a vast drawing board and surrounded by the numerous members of his family, all working like beavers.

'You ask me,' he said, 'when I first came to England. Actually, in 1891. I started my business life at the age of fourteen in a Paris studio. Although I had won a scholarship for the School of Arts, my father insisted that I should learn a craft and thus be sure of a living – hence my joining the Chromolithographic trade. When I was about fifteen years old, some artists who had just been to London came to the studio where I was apprenticed and said that even a youngster such as I could earn his living there, so unskilled were the rank and file amongst the lithographic artists in the England of those days. I was soon off to London where I arrived without any knowledge of the language or any idea of where to go. To my surprise – for in those days the English had a poor reputation for amiability on the Continent – I found so many charming people who helped me that I soon got a good job as a journeyman and have never looked back since.'

'And you came to like the English?' said I.

'Yes. Certainly, to go to England in those days was for a Frenchman a great adventure; not far different from going to some wild and uncivilised country. Perhaps I came to love England and its people because I found how different they were from what I had expected – so peaceful, so kind, so friendly.'

'And when did you first become interested in photo-lithography?'

'About 1905. Up to that time, very little was known about the subject. Pioneer work was being done principally in the provinces, and when an opportunity came for me to go to Leeds in 1910, I jumped at the opportunity. But the real success of these new methods did not materialise until after 1918. Since that date, my whole concern has been to improve the methods of lithographic reproduction. I think I can fairly claim to have done as much as any man in the country to develop these new processes and I am still striving for better things.'

'And when did you first become connected with John Waddington Ltd?'

'Ah! That was the great event of my business life, my meeting with Mr Victor Watson. I joined up with him in 1920 and have since done my small best to support him in his tremendous task of building up the firm of John Waddington Ltd.'

'And outside your business, Mr Vauvelle, have you any other interests in life?'

'Well, I can't say I am interested in sport. When I was a young man, in France sport was regarded as being an interest only suitable for people with no brains and I am afraid that I have never quite lost that view. In my youth, however, I was a very enthusiastic cyclist and that interest was transferred to motoring some twenty-odd years ago. I am also a very keen gardener, my special interest being the cultivation of orchids.'

So I left Mr Vauvelle amongst his cameras and dark rooms and the other implements of the fascinating trade of which he is, without question, the leading exponent in the country.

APPENDIX C

Ralph B. Stephens (RB) was a partner in Potter Stephens, the noted stockbrokers in Leeds, and was a director of many companies. He was associated with Waddingtons for nearly fifty years, and eventually became chairman. His knowledge of finance and business affairs was of tremendous importance to Victor Watson, especially in the early days. His brother, Cyril Stephens, became company secretary and he was followed in that job by Peter Stephens. RB died in 1953.

I also remember Frederick Eley, who was a forceful man. My mother disliked him because he was arrogant and called my grandfather 'Watson', not so much as an equal but as a subordinate. But my grandfather said that Eley had saved Waddingtons by lending the National Provincial Bank's money to the derelict business. (This is against the law nowadays and was questionable in 1913!) And my grandfather said that Eley was very helpful in the finance side in those early days. Eley's 'letter' to the company magazine in 1930 ran as follows:

FELLOW READERS,

Mr Victor Watson's letter in the March magazine is full of inspiration and encouragement. To me, strangely enough, its appearance was a coincidence, because for some time I have had in mind the idea of giving you, through the same medium, the little story of my association with Waddingtons.

Many of you, perhaps, have never heard of me, some of you will know me by sight through my occasional visits to the works, and quite a number it is my privilege to have personal acquaintance of. To one and all, however, I extend that symbol of friendship which appears so appropriately on the outward cover of our magazine, and I wish to add, what I am sure is pretty well recognised, that one of the first considerations of my colleagues and myself on the Board has been the welfare of the staff, to know that you are happy in your work and surroundings, and to feel that you are giving of your best in the right spirit.

Now for my narrative, and at the outset I shall surprise most of you, probably all, by telling you that I became acquainted with the business as far back as twenty-seven years ago, or two years more than Mr Victor Watson; indeed, I presume I shall be correct in laying claim to longer association than anyone on the books today; a fact of which I am truly proud in view of the important position which the company now holds in its particular lines of industry.

Going Back Twenty-Seven Years.

I am giving no secrets away at this lapse of time when I tell you that in 1903 I was manager of the bank where Mr John Waddington, the then sole proprietor, kept his account. Like many young concerns, the business needed help in the shape of an overdraft, and my bank by this means undoubtedly played an important part in Waddingtons' infancy; indeed, but for this there might have been no story to relate.

All went well for a time, save for a little steadily increasing overdraft, until one day Mr Waddington came to interview me with a decidedly dejected look, far removed from the optimistic smile which his pleasant face usually carried.

The Shadow of Bankruptcy.

He was accompanied by a professional gentleman, an accountant and stranger to me, who made himself spokesman by informing me that there was serious trouble and pressure from creditors, and that a Deed of Assignment had been executed, which even the lay mind will appreciate spelt bankruptcy and ruin. I was, to say the least, annoyed at this unexpected turn of events, because, as the bank was the largest creditor, I should in common courtesy have been consulted before such drastic steps were entered upon.

I firmly refused to agree to the measures proposed, and called for an up-to-date statement of affairs so that I could see for myself whether the business, very small then, was worthy of fighting for to keep it in being, despite what I knew to be the weakness, viz. its bad debts out of proportion to the profit and turnover. I was satisfied that there was the nucleus of a future, if capital could be found, and control assured of sound direction. A small private limited company was formed, share capital, not large, was forthcoming, and shortly afterwards Sir Arthur Peake and Mr Edgar Lupton joined the Board, as did Mr R. B. Stephens subsequently.

The 'Star Turn of the Piece' appears.

In passing I must pay tribute to these gentlemen, who in fair weather and foul have stood by the company financially and otherwise.

Later on Mr John Waddington left, and the 'Star Turn of the Piece' appeared in the person of Mr Victor Watson. You know the history since, that despite difficulties which have been many and recurring, the business has been one of steady progress from strength to strength, crowned, if one may say so, by the acquisition and remodelling of the Wakefield Road site at great outlay and cost – works of which we are indeed proud.

Without being boastful, and forgive me for stating it, I am sure that but for Mr Victor Watson on the practical side, and your humble servant on the finance, John Waddington Ltd would not have been in existence today.

Hope in the Future.

One word in conclusion. Our managing director's remarkable advancement from the bench to his present position, attained, despite early hardships, by sheer dogged determination and straightforwardness, is an example open to all to follow, and not only to follow, but, as the 'survival of the fittest', to attain. I for one express the hope that out of our own nursery, so to speak, we shall train up and produce those who will competently and honourably conduct the affairs of the company with the flag flying, long after some of us are no more.

FREDK. ELEY

APPENDIX D

When Doug Brearley wrote this history in about 1973, the Keighley process was still secret and hardly anybody was allowed to visit the works. The process was my father's brainchild and involved a reel of board just three cards wide on equipment specially made by Beasley French of Bristol. Harold Beasley and Gordon French had both left E. S. and A. Robinson's subsidiary, Strachan and Henshaw, to start a company making machines to produce paper bags at very high speed. Both Harold and Gordon were very good engineers, and after trials and tribulations and much help from Norman Watson and his assistants, they created a production line which started with a large reel of board, eight inches wide, then a small gravure cylinder machine for the backs of the cards, then a machine with four large printing cylinders with eighteen printing blocks on each (yellow, red, blue and black), then a varnisher and then a drying process, which had the reel going up and down the whole height of the old mill in Keighley, through the floors for ages until the inks were dry. Finally, there were separate calendering and punching processes.

The process, when it eventually ran smoothly, was a world beater. Fred Harrison and Clifford Brown were in charge and it was a superb operation.

APPENDIX E

26 May 1926

Dear Mother,

I am afraid you will think I have been rather negligent, but all the time the strike was on I hadn't a minute to sit down and write to anybody. We had a terrible time here, we kept about thirty girls in the place for ten days and a few men and about twenty-five apprentices. Mr Watson had beds from Longleys fixed up in the canteen for the men, and in the board room for the girls and Miss Childs, Mrs Talbot (a lady forewoman) Ivy, Jessie and myself slept in the room where we do gilt edging, and we five had to cook meals for about seventy people. We had to get up at 6.30 to cook bacon and eggs for the multitude, then the ordinary cook came in about 9 o'clock and she looked after the dinner but we had to stay in the canteen all the evening and help to entertain and then get the supper ready and wash everything up afterwards, so you can see how busy we were. All our people went out on strike except these few and on the first day of the strike we had about a thousand people outside our factory howling like a lot of lunatics. All the same, although it was hard work, we had some fun out of it all, we have a piano in the canteen and they danced most evenings and we had two ping pong sets and a gramophone so I think they all enjoyed themselves, a lot of them didn't want to go home anyway when it was over, I'll bet they had never had such good meals in their lives or slept under better conditions, some of them of course (particularly the girls) are filthy and no matter what you do they would never be any better. I would rather have had twice as many boys to look after as those girls, the boys were far better behaved and would do as they were told and were much tidier and everything, but the girls were most unruly and we never had one girl come into the kitchen to volunteer to help with the washing up, but we had at least four boys to help to wash up every night and they quite enjoyed it too. The girls in the works have called the office girls everything, snobs and goodness knows what but it was the office girls who looked after them, and it just shows you what people like that would be really like if the positions were reversed, the world wouldn't be worth living in, if the working-class, ignorant people had lots of money and better positions, they would be the biggest snobs out. I have learnt more about politics and been deeper into the actual things during this strike than ever before and I know this much, I wouldn't like to live in a world where they were all Socialists. Some people can't rule people without bullying them. The way these girls in the works treated us, just as if we were dirt and were there to wait on them hand and food without even a 'thank you'. I never heard one girl say 'thank you' or 'please', and one of the girls, about sixteen or seventeen she was, one night said to me 'get me a knife Ruby'. While girls of my own age in the office call me Miss Hawker, this cheeky little imp was so familiar and never said 'please' at all, so I took no notice until she asked again and then I said, 'Oh were you speaking to me' and gave her a gentle hint in manners, and another boy, about twenty, a big fat greasy looking individual came in one morning in the kitchen (the kitchen by the way has 'PRIVATE' written on the door but he scorned to look at that) and he said 'I want some dip'. We were absolutely disgusted with a lot of them, there were just a few nice ones that you could pick out here and there.

Mr Watson of course was heartbroken when all his workpeople left him and it has made him very very bitter, and you can quite understand his feelings when you think how he has worked and slaved to give these men work to do and his motto has always been 'No slack time' and whenever our men have had nothing much to do, they have <u>never</u> been sent home, and some of them have been here for years and just simply walked out of the place. This firm has lost £5000 owing to the strike to say nothing of the loss of trade, and I can't possibly see how a general strike could help the miners, the trade of this country will be put back again, and in business mother you realise that it is trade that keeps a country going, we want as much trade as we can get don't we to employ people. They don't seem to see that the more trade we get the more people will be employed, and as somebody said here 'How can ruining a printer help a miner?', and the miners don't care about everybody coming on strike to help them!

Why, lots of the girls and apprentices here, their fathers were miners so why in the world did they let their children go on working? Another thing, did you know that about four or five miners had applied to the railway office in Leeds for jobs and were set on? If it wasn't so tragic for some people it would be humorous wouldn't it?

Of course I know that lots of firms are not like Waddingtons, they don't all treat the workpeople like we do, and in Norman's department it was practically a non-Union department but a lot of his girls went out just because they were frightened. It might interest you to know that Brotherton's daughter (he is Labour MP for South Leeds) worked in Norman's department and she got them all to strike, and mind you, these girls are paid the Union rates of wages although they are not in a Union. The reason that this department is now strictly non-Union is because a lot of the girls work on what we call the 'bonus system' which means to say that if they do so much more work than is usually allotted to them, they are paid bonus accordingly. This of course makes them work harder which is what we want and incidentally it is better for themselves, they are glad of it, and Mr Watson has told them that the more bonus they earn the better he will be pleased. That girl Brotherton was a perfect devil, she was out here every day trying to get the girls out and causing mischief all round.

I know you are a great believer in Unions, I am not, I never quite understood it before but I quite agree that they have done a lot of good and they are necessary but they shouldn't rule the country should they? And I don't think they were right in bringing everybody out on strike.

Well, anyway, it is all over now but I do wish you hadn't put me in that Federation, it has been money wasted all these years and here I go on paying 6d. a week and I expect I shall eventually get a tenth of it back, if that, and if Mr Watson knew I expect I'd be sacked on the spot, to say nothing of losing my future husband. Raymond says he thinks I ought to tell Norman, but after I have helped them all this strike it will look so rotten won't it. And besides if I resign where do I get my insurance card from and wouldn't they find out? I've been thinking of going to see Mrs Arnott about it but I'd like to hear what you say first.

I have been to Pateley Bridge this holiday with the Watson family and Mr and Mrs Jack Spencer (Fanny Gregg) and the two children. It was just what I wanted, we stayed at a big house just on the outskirts of Pateley Bridge and the view was absolutely gorgeous, it is right at the top of a hill, and you look right down into the valley and right across the other side, it is very hilly but most beautiful. Really speaking, I prefer the north country to the south and it suits me much better, it is much more bracing. When I am down in Beckford I like the country and all that but I can't seem to get my lungs properly full of the air and it makes me feel awfully lazy. They were awfully nice people at the house, a widow and two daughters looked after us and her name was 'Mrs Waddington' – wasn't that funny? Tizzle went with us too and I was glad about that because she doesn't get anywhere much. You would love the country round there if you could stand the hills, and I'm sure it would brace you both up.

We haven't heard from Len for a long time, and I don't know whether he has been down to see you or not, I hope so.

Well mother after all this I think you will have your head full won't you, and you will think your daughter has turned into a rank Tory, but don't you believe it, I can quite see all your Labour views and all the rest of it but I don't see how you can see all points when you have not actual experience now can you? You only see one side, you don't see the point of view of all these top men, and you wouldn't believe how human and sympathetic they were, I am in constant touch with lots of these men in Leeds (through Mr Watson of course) and I find myself unconsciously taking their part and turning things over in my mind about right and wrong, they are not the money-grabbers that the people dub them, they don't make the huge profits that people believe, and some of them are far worse off financially than their own workpeople because they have to live up to their positions more. I'm glad I've got to be a private businessman's secretary, you have no idea how interesting it is and how strange it is to look on both sides of a question. I do think Raymond made a mistake in coming out on strike, he has lost his opportunity there absolutely.[1] If he had stayed in, it wouldn't have passed unnoticed and I'll bet that would have been just the step towards the promotion that he is always wanting, I don't think he'll ever get any further now, they will treat him just the same as all the men and not recognise him at all, I think he was a perfect fool, his opportunity was staring at him and he missed it, and although the men are making a fuss of him for coming out with them, they will soon be criticising him as usual and what can they do for his future, or what do they care? I was a bit surprised when he came out because if he had offered his services, they would have seen

---

1 Raymond, Ruby's brother, was working for a railway company at the time of the strike. Later on he joined Waddingtons as a playing card and games sales representative.

that he wasn't victimised, I'm convinced of that. Of course I have never said anything to him, he resents any advice you are willing to give, he thinks it is degrading to accept advice from his sister I expect, I don't see why it should be, but he does resent it, he resents it if you find fault with him in any way, he hasn't the sense to see that if you weren't fond of him you wouldn't bother to tell him at all.

I really must close now and get down to work. You never feel like work after a holiday do you? By the way, are you coming up this summer or do you want me to come down at Bank Holiday? Norman of course wants me to go to Blackpool with them at Bank Holiday but I haven't committed myself yet, I consult you first.

With very much love to Dad and yourself.

Your loving daughter
Ruby

APPENDIX F

(RELATES TO CHAPTER SEVEN)

Monopoly sets have mostly been based on capital cities. The first and most important exception is the original USA edition which was based on Atlantic City, a seaside resort near to Philadelphia. The reason? Well, most cities in the USA have numbers for the streets. In New York City there are famous thoroughfares like Fifth Avenue, Madison Avenue and 42nd Street, but they are the exceptions and there would not be enough well known streets with names to complete a Monopoly board. Atlantic City does have names for its streets though, which made it far more suitable for finding Monopoly locations. Outside North America the London board is the best known, with names like Piccadilly, Fleet Street, Bond Street and Mayfair.

At present there are not only examples of special editions based on a multitude of cities, but also mutations such as the Harley Davidson Monopoly, Star Wars Monopoly and the very successful Simpson's Monopoly.

In 1989 an early special edition was the Limited edition, which was appropriately based on Leeds where Monopoly in England was made from 1936 onwards. We had the idea of a Leeds edition to raise money for charity. I chose the sites, having first consulted customers in the tap room of the Victoria behind the Town Hall. I had Robert Maxwell in jail to start with but got cold feet and put myself in instead. Waddingtons set about producing it. But at Hasbro (who owned the rights) there was no enthusiasm. The Hasbro fold wanted to do a Berlin Wall edition instead. So I went cold on our Leeds idea, but then I found that our works had gone a long way down the road of preparing for a run. So I wondered what I could do to publicise it, and I thought of the Lord Mayor's charity. I put the idea to the Lord Mayor (Les Carter) who agreed to join in the launch which we did for Yorkshire Television's Calendar. The story also appeared in the *Yorkshire Evening Post*.

Next morning we had a queue at the works at Rothwell. Claire Palmer phoned me to ask what we should do. I had arranged a run of 500 and a selling price of £25. I said to Claire, 'stop selling them; say that there are just a few left and that people will have to write in for them.' We then sold the balance at higher prices, squeezing extra cash out of the well off for the Lord Mayor's charity. The Lord Mayor sold them too and used the sets as auction and raffle prizes. In the end the total raised was over £18,000. (Those who got them at £25 were very lucky.) I gave the Lord Mayor number one.

APPENDIX G

(RELATES TO CHAPTER TWELVE)

WARBURGS' SHAREHOLDING IN WADDINGTONS

Notes written by Victor Watson, 10 January 1985:

Warburgs' first shares for the Mercury Fund were acquired in the summer of 1983 during the bid. I think we became aware of the holding in early September.

On 5 September 1983 I called to see Charles Cavanagh, the fund manager, and he had with him Leonard Licht, his managing director. They said that they had 175,000 shares and that they had accepted the BPCC bid. I did my stuff as best as I could and followed it by telephoning him the next day. It was no use; I could not persuade them to withdraw.

I called on Charles Cavanagh on 17 April 1984. He included two other people in the meeting, one of whom was Carole Galley who I later learned was Charles's boss. At the time we thought that the Warburgs holding was 218,000, but Charles informed me that they had 6.5%, which made it about 470,000 shares. By now the shares were held in the Mercury Fund but also in Nutraco and a large part of Nutraco was the Sainsbury's pension fund. I asked him if they had discretion with regard to the Sainsbury's part; he said 'yes', but in a bid they would get Sainsbury's approval before assenting. They said that they were middle ground shareholders and would sell if the price was right. Charles was friendly enough. The others were not.

Charles Cavanagh came to the AGM on 20 July 1984. They did not vote either way at the meeting and I had an argument with him about it. He said that he did not want to interfere in a difference of opinion between us and Maxwell. I said that I could not understand his attitude as we were suggesting things which were beneficial to the company of which he was a shareholder.

On 7 August 1984 Charles visited our head office in Leeds. I was away. He was impressed with what he saw and congratulated everybody on the results, but said that he thought Maxwell would bid again and that in buying Waddingtons shares, he could not lose.

On 26 October 1984 I telephoned Charles Cavanagh. He said that it would depend on price.

On 30 October 1984 we thought that the Warburgs shares amounted to 1,102,000, being 12.5%.

On 26 November 1984 I asked David Perry to speak to Cavanagh as a result of David's advice to me that Cavanagh is slightly anti family businesses. Charles said to David, 'We are hard-nosed businessmen; we will sell if someone comes along.' He was hinting about a white knight but also suggesting that he would be prepared to unload the shares. He went on to say that he would prefer a direct approach rather than through a merchant bank.

On 4 December 1984 Roy Dearden of Cazenoves telephoned me to say that Warburgs were aggressive with their holding and seemed to be expecting Cazenoves to place it. I thought at the time that Warburgs had built up a strategic holding and could now see that if the bid failed and Maxwell's shares were placed, there would be nothing to do with that strategic holding. It seemed obvious that they were going to use their position to the best advantage.

At this time Christopher Eugster was in touch with David Sainsbury in the hope that we could persuade Sainsbury's to instruct Warburgs not to accept the offer.

On 5 December 1984 David and I discussed the Warburgs holding with Kleinwort Benson and Cazenoves, and while we were meeting Roy Lister of Cazenoves telephoned to say that Leonard Licht of Warburgs had been talking to Julian Cazalet about it. We discussed possible ways to buy out part or all of the Warburgs holding, including using some of my friends. That day I did actually telephone Neil Pullan to see if he would help once again.

On the morning of 6 December 1984 Kleinworts met to consider putting up more than £1 million to help with the purchase of Warburgs' stage. That same morning David Perry and I visited Warburgs and met Charles Cavanagh, Carole Galley and Julia Hobert. This was the first time that we realised that Carole Galley was a director of the bank and Charles's boss. In my diary I described her as, 'looking as if she had been chiselled from the finest quality Italian marble.' We did our stuff but Charles reminded us again that money was the only thing that concerned them. He said, 'I am not paid to take your employees into consideration.' He said that they had a strategic stake and would only sell it as one lot. He said that they would accept a price well above 500 and mentioned 535. I said that if they would not accept 510 from someone else, they would presumably not accept 500 from BPCC. He did not comment on that. At this stage it was Eugster's idea to buy part of Warburgs' stage at, say, 505. We agreed that if they bought Warburgs shares and lost on them, then an extra fee could be paid, and a figure of up to £125,000 was mentioned. On the basis that with the fee that we had just agreed at £175,000, an extra £125,000, making a total of £300,000, would not seem out of the way. At this stage we also discussed the possibility of trying to buy Lonrho's shares and leaving Warburgs in the cold. We decided to leave the whole thing for a day or two anyway.

Eugster had maintained contact with David Sainsbury in regard to the 325,000 shares that Warburgs had for the Sainsbury's pension fund.

On 10 December 1984 we discussed the Warburgs stake again and Eugster explained that if Kleinworts bought any part at a high price, it would upset the loyal institutions.

On 11 December 1984 Anthony Forbes telephoned to say that Warburgs had been on unofficially to say that they would sell the lot at 520. With Kleinworts they formed a plan to find people to take the shares at 510 and then go to see Warburgs about it. In order to marshal the firepower, Anthony Forbes asked if I would speak to Stock Beech. I said that I would rather that he did it, which was a wise move as Cazenoves and Kleinworts thought that Stock Beech had let the cat out of the bag, although they had to admit that Stock Beech came up trumps in finding shareholders.

On the evening of 11 December Christopher Eugster joined me at the Grandfield Rorke Collins cocktail party specifically to pass on to me the good news that the whole of Warburgs' stake had been moved on at a price of 507.5. He and Julian Cazalet had been to see Licht and two others.

The total number of shares sold by Warburgs was 1,279,500, being 14.64% of the Waddingtons shares.

VHW, 10 January 1985.

When I read such things as the Cadbury Report, I remember my experiences, which have taught me not to think of all the shareholders as being in the category of owners of the business. When some shareholders are waiting to bid for you and others are waiting to cash in on a bid, it is barmy to treat them as if they are the owners of the business, interested in its long-term future and survival.

INDEX

3 Woodhouse Cliff
 5

Aberforth Partners
 161
Aberforth Unit Trust
 161
Abrahams, Michael D.
 132, 135, 138, 139, 140, 154, 157, 159
Active Value Fund Managers Ltd
 159
advertisers
 12, 14, 20, 25, 31
Alf Cooke Ltd
 91
Allen, Bert
 31
Allen, Jim
 25
Almscliffe Crag
 112
Altenburg and Stralsunder
 118
Amalgamated Playing Card Company, the
 92–93

Angel Islington
 80
Ansbacher
 142, 146
Anspach, Ralph
 79, 82
Anti-Monopoly
 79, 82
Arnold, Olav
 112, 129
Asquith, Peter
 128
Australasian Publication Company
 14
Australia
 14, 21, 68, 86, 87
Auxiliary Board of directors
 19

Bailey, Martin
 123
Bain Dawes
 135
Ball, Charles (Kleinwort Benson)
 99, 100

Ballantyne, Hanson and Co.
44
Bank of England, the
32
  – banknotes, Waddingtons' production of
32, 33, 36
Barribal
11
Barrow, Simon
126, 138, 138, 139, 140
Barton, Ranny
v, 81, 82
Barton, Robert
79, 80, 81
Bear Street, London (premises at)
10
Beasley French & Co. Ltd
30, 90, 174
Beasley, Harold
67, 90, 174
Beckett, William
128
Bengers Ltd
31
Benson, Sid
27
Berlin
86, 114, 180
Berlin Wall, the
180
Birds Eye
97
Birkman, Lew
98
Birmingham
23, 121
Bishopsgate
144

Blades, Mr
39
Blaydon Dairies
30
Blue Ribbon (prize)
12
Board of directors, Waddingtons
8, 11, 12, 30, 40, 43, 44, 46, 47, 49, 50, 51, 100, 105, 120, 124, 125, 132, 137, 142, 159, 160, 162–163, 166, 167, 172, 173
Board of Trade, the
35–36, 113
Bob's Yr Uncle (game)
77
Boosales, Jim
83
Bootham School
65, 198
Bowater
108, 117, 153, 159, 161
Bower, Tom
113
Bowes, Christopher J. L. (finance director)
105, 110, 111, 115, 129, 135, 156
Bradford, West Yorkshire
1, 2, 34, 90, 129
Bradley, Harry
26, 97
Brain, Philip
154
Brand Packaging
118
Brandreth, Giles
150
Brearley, Douglas
7, 23, 77, 79, 80, 92, 95, 131, 135, 169, 174

Brett Litho of New York
    74
bridge (game)
    6, 15, 24, 68, 91, 92
Bridge Magazine
    92
Bristol
    22, 23, 30, 90, 97, 123, 174
Britannic Assurance Company, the
    121, 124, 125
British American Tobacco
    99
British Empire Exhibition, the
    15
British Printing and Communication
    Group (BPCC)
    105, 112, 113, 115, 119, 120–121,
    124, 126, 127, 128, 130, 137, 143,
    144, 145, 147, 150, 151, 156, 182,
    184
British Printing Industry Federation
    vii
British Steel
    144
British Vending Industries
    118
Broackes, Nigel
    83
Brough, Charlie
    13
Brough, Jim (manager)
    30
Brown, W. Anthony B.
    105, 135, 138
Brudenell, James, Earl of Cardigan
    5
Bryant and May
    50

Buccaneer (game)
    64, 80
Buckley, Martin
    118, 135, 156, 158, 159, 160,
    161, 162, 163
Bunhill Row, London
    91
Bunn, Jason
    87
Bunzl
    109
Burley Park railway station
    5
Burley Park, Leeds
    1, 5
Burrup and Matthieson
    122

Cadbury's
    34, 97
California Cutlery
    154
call-up to war
    31
Cambridge
    60
    – Cambridge University
    91, 198
Cameron, Douglas (director)
    9, 11, 12, 14, 20, 25, 31, 36
Camp Road, Leeds (premises at)
    7, 8, 10, 14, 48, 49
Campbell-Smith, Duncan
    146
Canada
    29, 30, 98, 107
    – Toronto
    30

Cardew, Anthony
    143
Cardigan Press
    (later RustCraft)
    5, 98
Carter, H. M. (director)
    8
Carter, Hugh
    99
Carter, Les (Lord Mayor of Leeds)
    180–181
Carthage Cup
    154
Cavanagh, Charles
    182–183
Cazalet, Julian
    146, 183, 184
Cazenoves
    108, 115, 122, 123, 135, 142, 146,
    183, 184
Central and Sheerwood
    109
Chadwick, Everard
    (lawyer, vice-chairman and chairman)
    67, 99, 100–101, 135
Chandos Street (premises at)
    60
Charge of the Light Brigade
    5
Charing Cross Road (premises at)
    55
Charles Goodall and Co. Ltd
    14, 89
    – absorbed by Thomas De La Rue
    and Co. Ltd
    12, 89
Charles Russell
    9, 42, 43

Chorley and Pickersgill
    155, 158
Churchill, Winston
    ix, 35, 36
    – *(Memoirs of the Second
    World War)*
    35
cigarettes
    – Woodbines
    23
    – Capstan
    23
    – Star
    23
    – Gold Flake
    23
cinema
    20, 95, 96, 142
Clare College, Cambridge
    112, 198
Clare House, Scotland Lane, Horsforth
    5, 64, 67, 68
Cluedo (Clue)
    81, 82, 118, 140, 157, 158
Cohen, Jack
    84
Comet Products
    154
Communisis
    ix, 153, 155, 162, 163
Compston, Lottie
    (later Barnard, then Wimble)
    64
Conisby Dene
    64, 67
Conqueror Typewriter Company, the
    12, 50
Continental Can
    109

Coors
    117
Cope Allman
    109
copyright issues
    14, 79
Cornish, Evan
    118
court proceedings
    14, 82, 130
Crabtrees
    65, 90–91
Craig, Gordon
    122, 123
Cramsie, Marc
    122
Cranston, Don
    98
Cranston, Fred
    98
cricket
    1, 5, 6, 51, 64, 68, 91
Crown Playing Cards
    93
Cups Illustrated
    154
Czechoslovakia
    113, 150

Daguerre, Louis J. M.
    74
Daily Mirror, the
    137, 142, 143, 146, 150
Daily Telegraph, the
    100, 116, 137
Dalton, Andrew
    135
Darrow, Charles B.
    28, 78, 79

Davidson Radcliffe
    109
Dawson, Elizabeth
    3
de la Pradelle, Raymond de Geoffrey
    143
De La Rue
    (Thomas De La Rue and Co. Ltd)
    – market competitors
    19, 89, 91, 92–93
    – sued Waddingtons
    14–15
    – cooperation with Waddingtons
    33–34, 36, 89, 90–93, 98, 99
Dearden, Roy (Cazenoves)
    108, 123, 124, 135, 183
Denmark
    29, 30
Dixon, George (company secretary)
    11
Dixon, Mr
    42, 166, 168
Dobson and Crowther
    118
Dobson, Clem
    31
Dodsworth, Ted
    18–19
Drakeford, Mr
    48, 49
DRG
    108
Driscoll, Mrs
    125
Dublin
    28
duty wrappers on playing cards
    15, 89, 92–93

E. S. and A. Robinson
    90, 174
Eagle Transfers
    99
Eastman, George
    74
Easy Money (game)
    79
Einson Freeman
    26
Eley, Frederick
    – bank manager
    8, 171–173
    – chairman
    11, 40, 46, 125
Elland Road, Leeds (premises at)
    9, 41, 42
Esselte
    108, 117
Eugster, Christopher
    146, 183, 184
Eureka
    98
Euston
    122
Evans, Mike
    154
Evening Standard, the
    127
Eversheds
    (see Hepworth and Chadwick)
    157
Ex-Cell-O Corporation, the
    95–96

F. and A. Parkinson of Guiseley
    26
Ferguson
    109

Field Son & Co. Ltd
    34
Finance (game)
    78, 79
Financial Times, the
    116, 126, 127, 144, 146, 157
Fine Art
    109
First World War
    9, 12, 13, 29, 41, 45, 46
Fisher Price
    140
Fisons
    159
Floral Street (premises at)
    10, 20, 44, 45
folding cartons
    21, 25, 26, 27, 28, 29, 35, 66, 97, 107, 153, 154, 157
    – glueing machines
    25
    – boxboard
    25, 26
Foley, Martin
    92–93
Forbes, Anthony
    122, 184
Forgrove Machinery Company, the
    30
Forrest, Joe
    37
Fox-Talbot, William Henry
    74
France
    29, 34, 46, 170
Fraser, Marten
    135

French, Gordon
    90, 174
Frost, David
    127

Gallaghers
    128
Galley, Carole
    182, 183–184
Gateshead (premises at)
    34, 36, 162
Gaunt, Norman
    95–96, 97, 105, 117, 154
General Mills
    79, 81, 82, 109, 117, 118, 140
    – takeover of Parker Brothers
    81, 82
General Strike, the (1926)
    15, 16–18, 52, 53–54, 175–177, 178–9
George Mann and Co. Ltd
    18
Gibson, Geoff
    135, 156, 158, 163
Gill, Eric
    114–115
Gilmour and Dean
    155, 157, 158
Glyndebourne
    113
Goodall and Son
    89
Goodall and Suddick
    2, 44
Government, the
    21, 30, 31, 32, 34, 44, 45, 107
Grabsky, Mike
    87

Great Western Railway Company
    14
Great Wilson Street, Leeds (premises at)
    8, 9, 10, 11, 12, 38, 41, 44, 49, 52, 54, 55
Green Shield
    98
Greig, Miss
    42
Grieveson Grant
    142
Grimston, Len
    25
Grove, Josceline
    143
Guardian Royal Exchange
    124
Guardian, the
    117, 145
Guest, Jonathon
    135

Habourdin, Michel
    143
Hallmark Cards
    107
Hanson
    109
Hanson, Mr
    38
Hanwell, Richard
    111, 116, 149
Harrison, Fred
    (manager of Keighley factory)
    19, 65, 174
Harrison, Peter
    96
Harrison, Townsend and Co.
    5, 8, 38

Hartman, Carl. W and Louis M.
    29, 30
Harvey, John Martin
    8
Hasbro
    86, 93, 140, 157, 158, 161, 180
Headingley Cricket Club
    6, 68
Heffernan, John
    104, 116
Heinz
    28, 97
Hepworth and Chadwick, (solicitors)
    10, 100, 115, 135, 157
Herbert Smith
    115
Heseldine, Mr
    44
Hestair
    139
Hibbert, Ivy (née Wigglesworth)
    64
Hicks, Rupert
    29, 30
Hird, Mr
    38
Hirst, Alan
    116, 135
Hirst, Clarrie
    14, 17
HM Customs and Excise
    89, 92
HM Treasury
    34, 93
Hodgson, Norris
    135
Holbeck, Leeds
    6, 135

Holbrook, Gerry
    116
Hollowood, John
    159
Holmburg, Axel
    30, 96
Holt, James
    118
Honeysett, Peter
    135
Hope Mills, Water Lane (premises at)
    49
Hopple Plastics
    154
Horsforth
    5, 6, 64, 198
Horwood, Bill
    128
Hoskins, Ruth
    78, 79
House of Commons, the
    114
House of Questa, the
    137–138, 139, 141, 154, 158
Hunslet, Leeds
    6, 8, 12

Iceland
    84, 85
ICI Metals Ltd
    34, 36
Imperial Tobacco
    99
Independent Dairies
    30
International Paper Company, the
    96

Ireland
  2, 28
Izzi, Clem
  154

Jacobs, Greg
  86, 87
Jacobsen, Jeff
  83
Jani, Hans
  118
Jessell, Oliver
  83
jigsaw puzzles
  25, 26–27, 158
John Mansfield Group Ltd
  159, 160, 161
Johnsen and Jorgensen
  155
Jones, David
  159, 161, 162, 163
Jorgensen, John
  135, 155
Jupiter Asset Management
  128

Karno, Fred
  8
Keighley (premises at)
  15, 19, 65, 70, 90, 92, 174
  – as Lamonby Manufacturing Company
  65
Kenner
  82
Kenner Parker
  83

Killingbeck Hospital
  4
Kilroy, Howard
  118
King, Fred
  44
Kirkness, Chris
  122
Kleinwort Benson
  99, 100, 115, 122, 123, 126, 135, 138, 142, 143, 146, 183, 184

Lamert, Sidney
  90–91
Landor
  109
Lascelles, Lord
  12
Lauder, Andrew
  118
Layman, Dan
  78, 79
Lazards
  100
Le Blon, J. C.
  73
Leach, Sir Ronald
  113
Leasco
  113, 114
Leeds and Holbeck Building Society
  135
Leeds General Infirmary
  4
Leeds Grammar School
  4, 5, 64
Leeds Grand Theatre
  7

Leeds, West Yorkshire
   1, 2, 4, 5, 6, 7, 8, 9, 10, 11, 12,
   15, 19, 22, 23, 30, 31, 33, 34, 36,
   43, 45, 47, 48, 53, 63, 64, 68, 74,
   86, 90, 91, 92, 98, 115, 119, 122,
   125, 130, 132, 134, 135, 155, 157,
   158, 159, 161, 163, 165, 167, 170,
   171, 177, 178, 180, 183, 198
Lermer
   160
Lever Brothers
   25, 50
Lewenthal, Raymond
   98
Lewin, Bob
   74
Lexicon
   27, 77, 80, 93
Licht, Leonard
   182, 183, 184
Liechtenstein
   143, 146
Linpac
   108, 118, 156
Liquid Packaging
   96
Liss, David
   123
Lister, Roy
   183
Lockhart's
   60
London
   10, 15, 22, 28, 30, 33, 43, 44, 45, 52,
   53, 58, 59, 60, 66, 79, 80, 83, 85, 86,
   89, 91, 93, 112, 116, 122, 123, 127,
   130, 138, 142, 169, 180
   – City, the
   100, 113, 114, 115, 118, 138, 140,
   141, 145, 146, 158, 159

London and North Eastern Railway
   Company
   14
London Evening News
   83
London Savoy Theatre
   18
London School of Printing, the
   112
Lonrho
   109, 142, 143, 184
Loomis, Bernie
   82
Lord Rothermere
   144
Louis Marx
   26, 27
Low and Bonar
   109, 158
Lunn, Kenneth
   105, 135, 140, 153
Lupton, Edgar
   – chairman
   8, 10, 44, 165, 167, 168
   – director
   8, 10, 44, 46, 173
   – vice-chairman
   11, 46

M and G
   122, 123, 124, 146
MacMillan, Harold
   114
Mail on Sunday, the
   123, 146
Mair, John
   85
Malbert, David
   83

INDEX

Mardon International
  97, 99
  – takeover bid
  97
Marley
  160, 161
Martin, Jim
  99
Mason, Tony
  99
Master Printers' Federation
  10, 19, 52
Matchbox Toys
  140
Mattel
  140
Maxwell, James Clerk
  74
Maxwell, Robert (Jan Ludwig Hoch)
  ix, 105, 108, 112, 113, 114, 115,
  116, 117, 118, 119, 120, 121,
  125–126, 127, 128, 129-130,
  132, 137–139, 142, 143, 144–147,
  149–151, 153, 156, 157, 180, 183
  – background
  113–114
  – character
  113
  – and Leasco
  113–114
  – First bid (1983)
  114–120, 125–129
  – Second bid (1984)
  132, 137–147
  – acquires the *Daily Mirror*
  142, 143, 150
  – interviewed by David Frost
  127

  – press coverage and publicity
  116, 117, 126, 127, 137, 142, 143,
  145, 146, 149, 150
  – meeting with Victor Watson
  120
McArthur, John
  122, 126, 138–139, 140
McCarthy, Callum
  135
McClements, Robert
  v, vii
McCorquodale
  110, 162
McGregor, Ian
  144
Meccano Magazine
  98
Mercury Fund, the
  182
Messrs David Allen
  44
Metal Box
  96, 108, 119
Metal Closures
  109
Meyercord Decalcomania Company, the
  99
Middleton Park land purchase
  49
Midland Bank
  116, 135
Mills and Allen
  109
Milton Bradley
  79, 82, 140
miners
  16, 176–177
Misselbrook, Desmond
  99

197

Mitchell, Michael (director)
   155
Mobil
   117
Monopoly
   v, ix, 28, 64, 77–80, 81–83, 84,
   85–87, 100, 118, 140, 157, 158,
   161, 180
   – origins of
   28, 64, 78–79
   – brought to the UK
   77, 118
   – board sites
   79, 80, 85, 86, 180
   – threats to licence
   81–82, 100
   – National Championships
   84, 85
   – European Championships
   84
   – World Championships
   83, 86–87
   – special editions of
   180
Monte Carlo
   86
Moore, Charles
   31
Moortown Golf Club
   5, 92, 198
Morgan Grenfell
   118
Morley, Robert
   84
Morrison, Sir Ken
   132
Mortlocks, London
   30

Moss Empires Ltd
   16
Murdoch, Rupert
   137, 143
Musgrave, Mr
   53
Myerson, Brian
   159, 160, 161

Nalen, Craig
   81, 82
Nampak
   158
National Administration, the
   21
National Provincial Bank
   8, 46, 125, 171
NatWest Bank
   108, 115–116, 135, 144, 159
Nestlé
   124
No.1 Playing Cards
   92, 93
Noble Lowndes
   116, 135, 156
Nobles
   118
Norcross
   98, 100, 109, 161
Norman, Torquil
   157
Norton and Wright
   (see also Norton Opax)
   ix, 108, 111–112, 123
Norton Opax
   (see also Norton and Wright)
   112, 113, 116, 119, 120, 129,
   137, 149
Norwich Union
   124, 126–127, 128

Observer, the
    143, 146
Office of Fair Trading, the
    119
Oldham Co-Operative Society
    30
Orbanes, Phil
    v, 78, 79
    – *Monopoly®: The World's Most Famous Game and How it Got That Way*
    78
Ormond Printing Company, the
    28, 99
Orr, Michael
    158, 159, 160
Oval, the
    1

Palmer, Claire
    181
Parker Brothers
    28, 77, 78, 79, 80, 81–82, 83, 84, 117
Parker, George
    79
Peacock, William (director)
    8
Peake, Arthur Copson (Sir)
    – Leeds Solicitor
    8
    – director
    8, 46, 168
Pennsylvania
    78, 98, 28
pension scheme
    20, 117, 163
Pentos
    109

Pergamon Group, the
    114, 142, 145
Pergamon Holdings Foundation
    143
Pergamon Press
    142
Perry, David G. (managing director)
    v, 105, 107, 114, 120, 122, 126, 128, 133, 138, 139, 142, 150, 151, 153, 156, 157, 158, 183
Petty, Keith
    122
Petty, Ken
    112, 113, 119, 129
Phildrew Ventures
    160
Philips and Drew
    128
Phillips, Elizabeth (née Magie)
    28, 78, 79
Phillips, Marjorie
    80
plastic containers
    96, 97, 99, 111, 119, 139, 141, 153, 154, 160
Plastocan
    108
Plastona
    96, 108, 158
playing cards
    10, 11, 12–13, 14, 15, 17, 18, 20, 21, 22, 23, 24, 28, 32, 33, 34, 35, 65, 66, 74, 77, 89–90, 92, 93, 153, 158
    – 'Beautiful Britain' playing cards
    14
    – Wills' Playing Card Scheme
    20, 22–24, 77

– carton cutting and creasing machine
19–20
– gold edging
24
– shortage in Second World War
35–36
– punching processes in manufacture of
90, 174
– gravure process for
90, 174
– varnishing of
90
– calendering of
90, 174
PLM
117
polyester terephthalate tray technology
141
Post Office, the
154
postage stamps
74, 139, 153, 154
posters
7, 11, 15, 17, 18, 20, 21, 41, 44, 45, 66, 75, 99
– largest ever printed
15
Price Service
112
Price Waterhouse
115, 135, 143, 156
Prices and Incomes Policy, the
107
Printers' Charitable Corporation
143
Printers' strike
52–53

printing processes, machines and materials
– lithography
13, 74, 75
– offset lithography
11, 13
– mezzotints
73
– engraving and intaglio
74
– chromolithography
74, 75
– photolithography
75, 170
– lithographic machinery
8, 18
– Quad Crown litho. Machines
41
– step and repeat machines
14
– letterpress printing
8, 90
– forme-making
25
– wooden type
8
– steel cylinders and steel beds
18
– type-setting equipment
19
– rotary press
75
– reel fed press
75, 90
– lithographic artists
74, 75, 169
– lithographic stones
13, 75

– nitric acid
13
– paper
9, 15, 25, 29, 30–31, 32, 35, 45, 64, 66, 73, 75, 95, 97, 163, 174
– ink
15, 73, 74, 90, 97, 163, 174
Printing World
161
PrintYorkshire
vii
Pritchard, Charles
116
profits
20, 22, 24, 29, 81, 110, 145, 160, 162, 178
Prudential Assurance Company
154
Prudhoe, Claxton
34, 92
Pullan, Neil
128, 183

Queen Elizabeth II
93, 133

Rank, J. Arthur
95
ration boxes
34
Rawcliffe, Keith
135
Rawlings, John
144
Readers Digest
86–87
Reckitts
20, 50

redundancies
107, 114–115, 116, 144
Reeds
108
Remnant, the Hon. Philip
135
Render, Sam
25
Rexam (also see Bowater)
153, 159, 161, 162
Richard Edward of London
93
Rockley, Lord
123
Rogan, Harold
108, 118
Rose Forgrove Ltd
105
Rothschilds
123
Rothwell (premises at)
24, 181
Rowland, Tiny
142
Rowntrees
97, 124
Royal Academy of British Printing
12
Royal Warrant
93
Royal Warrant Holder's Association, the
93, 198
Rundle, Ted
135
RustCraft
5, 98

Sainsbury's
    127, 146, 182, 183, 184
Salisbury, Frank
    131
Samuel Montagu
    111
Sanderson and Clayton
    118
Satona Ltd
    26, 29, 31, 95–96
    – Satona waxed cartons
    26, 28, 29, 30, 31, 32, 34, 95–96
Schweppes
    95, 96, 98, 154
Scottish Amicable
    124, 128
Second World War
    ix, 5, 20, 26, 28, 30, 31
Selby Wilson
    21
Senefelder, Alois
    73–74
Shakeshaft, Peter
    135
shareholders
    8, 95, 100, 101, 103, 104, 105,
    110, 111, 112, 114, 115, 118,
    119, 120–121, 122, 123, 124,
    125, 126, 127, 130, 137, 142,
    143, 144, 146, 149, 153, 154,
    156, 158, 159, 161, 162, 182,
    184, 185
shares
    11, 18, 29, 83, 100, 106, 110,
    111, 115, 118, 120, 121, 123,
    125, 126, 128, 129, 137, 141,
    142, 143, 146, 159, 160, 161,
    182, 183, 184

Shop Missus (game)
    77
Schroder Ventures
    160
silk maps
    34
Singer and Friedlander
    124
SLADE
    114
Slater, Bob
    41, 42
Slater, Jim
    83, 84
Smurfit
    108, 118
Smurfit, Michael
    118
Snowden, Philip
    21
Snowden, Ros
    159
Sotheby's
    119
South Africa
    64
    – Johannesburg
    30
Spears
    139
Spencer, Fanny (née Spencer)
    64
Sperry and Hutchinson
    99
Spielberg, Stephen
    82
Spink, George (assistant manager)
    9, 10, 19
    – elected to Auxiliary Board
    19

Stable, Owen QC
 113
staff salaries
 21, 42
Standard Cheque
 162
stationery trade
 14, 23, 27, 92, 99, 153
Steinberg, Saul
 114
Stembridge and Co. Ltd
 19, 21, 27, 30
Stembridge, James A.
 19, 30
 – (elected to Auxiliary Board)
 19
Stephens, Cyril (Company Secretary)
 – director
 36
 – company secretary
 171
Stephens, Peter (company secretary)
 v, 8, 105, 122, 125, 130, 135, 156, 171
Stephens, Ralph Bernard
 9, 40, 41, 42, 43, 46, 54, 70, 170
 – stockbroker
 8, 10
 – director
 10, 46, 48, 165, 167, 168
 – joint managing director
 11, 40
 – chairman
 170
Stock Beech
 123, 184
Stock Exchange, the
 105, 111, 127, 128, 143, 161

Stoke Newington, North London (premises at)
 10, 20, 46–48
Stone, Arthur
 135
Stones of Banbury
 23
Strachan and Henshaw
 174
Strand Imperial, the
 60
Street, George
 57, 58, 59
Strip Tease (game)
 77
Sunday Telegraph, the
 143, 146
Sunday Times, the
 143, 146
Swanson, Don
 82
Sweden
 25, 29
Sykes, David
 135, 157
Syrad, John
 118

T. and T. Gill
 115
takeover bids
 ix, 97, 103–104, 115, 139
Takeover Panel
 105, 120, 123, 126, 127, 137, 145, 146
Takeover rules of 1983
 105, 120, 127, 137, 138, 143, 161

Tanzer, Eric
    112, 113
Tapperell, Geoff
    99
Target
    123
taxes
    21, 78, 103, 104, 110, 138,
    140, 158
Taylor, Fred
    12, 15
Taylor, Hugh
    24
Taylor, Ronnie
    24
Termans, Dana
    87
The Landlord's Game (game)
    78, 79
theatre posters
    7, 17
theatre programmes
    98
thermoforming
    96, 99, 154
Thomas Preston
    118
Thornhill, Dewsbury
    1
Thornton, Clive
    142
Thoy, Dennis
    135
Thyne Junior, William
    29
Thyne, Richard G.
    29

Thynes of Edinburgh
    29
Tilling
    109
Times, the
    145, 146
Toffler, Alvin
    103
Top Trumps (game)
    158
Town Hall, Leeds
    3, 180
Trade Unions
    16, 17, 30, 52, 54, 107, 114, 117,
    119, 177
    – power curbed by Conservative
    Government
    107
trading stamps
    98
Treger, Julian
    159, 160, 161
Tribe and Son
    10
Tribe, George
    10
TUC (Trades Union Congress)
    21
Tucker, David
    123–124
Tugwell, John
    116
Turner, Walter
    38
Typographical Society
    53

INDEX

Ulrick, Terry
  161
Unemployment
  21
Unilever Companies
  20, 25, 109, 110, 123
Union Mills, Dewsbury Road, Leeds
  (premises at)
  9, 42, 43, 49
United Printers
  98
United States of America
  19, 21, 25, 26, 50, 81, 180
  – Salem, Massachusetts
  28, 77, 78, 80
  – Atlantic City
  78, 79, 80, 86, 87, 180
  – Minneapolis
  81
  – Washington D. C.
  83, 84, 85
  – New York
  26, 28, 74, 80, 86, 98, 143, 180
  – New Jersey
  117
University of Leeds, the
  132, 198

Vaduz, Liechtenstein
  146
Valentines of Dundee
  98, 99, 107, 156
Van Den Bergh
  96, 119, 154
Vaughan, Steve
  163
Vauvelle, Achille
  11, 12, 13, 169–170

Vickers Business Forms
  137, 139, 154, 158
Victoria cricket ground
  5
Videomaster
  107

W. H. Smith
  99
Waddington Business Forms
  (also see Vickers Business Forms)
  158
Waddington Team Magazines
  37–55
Waddington, John (director)
  7, 8, 9, 38, 40, 48, 57, 61, 69, 165,
  166, 167, 168, 172, 173
Waddingtons Games Ltd
  93, 118, 131, 158
Waddingtons North America (WNA)
  154
Wade Lane (premises at)
  38
Wakefield Road (premises at)
  12, 14, 15, 16, 17, 19, 22, 30, 34,
  36, 49, 50, 64, 68, 134, 157, 173
Waldorf Hotel
  66, 91
Walker, Patrick
  124
Wallis, Stuart
  159, 161
war work
  34
  – (confidential)
  32
Warburgs
  145–146, 182–184

205

Watford
> 127, 144, 146

Watford Observer, the
> 144

Watkinson, Len
> 18

Watmoughs
> 124, 129, 137

Watson, Beric
> 64, 65, 66, 67, 107, 131, 139, 155

Watson, Elizabeth (née Peace)
> 1, 2

Watson, Eric
> 3

Watson, Ethel (née Dawson)
> 2, 3, 4, 5

Watson, Horace
> 2, 10, 47, 48, 66, 67, 92

Watson, John G. B. (MP for Skipton)
> v, 105, 110, 128, 135, 138, 139, 150, 155

Watson, Muriel
> 4, 64, 67

Watson, Norman (chairman)
> 2, 3, 4, 5, 12, 13, 19, 22, 23, 25, 27, 29, 30, 32, 35, 54, 77, 80, 97, 131 134, 174, 177, 179

Watson, Ruby (née Hawker)
> 5, 64, 175–179

Watson, Sheila
> 100, 112, 113, 146

Watson, Thomas
> 1, 2

Watson, Victor Hugo (1878–1943)
> 1–6, 7, 8, 9, 10, 11, 12, 13, 15, 17, 20, 22, 23, 26, 27, 29, 30, 31 33, 36, 37–55 57–61, 69, 70, 73, 75, 77, 79, 80, 89, 91, 131

– background
> 1–4

– apprenticeship
> 2, 4

– lithographer
> 8–9

– manager
> 9

– director
> 10

– managing director
> 11

– death of
> 36

Watson, Victor Hugo
> 100, 108, 120, 127, 132, 133, 135, 138, 139, 140, 141, 149, 184

– childhood
> 63–68

– managing director
> 81

– action to keep Monopoly licence
> 81–82

– defence against Norton and Wright
> 111–112

– fight against Maxwell in 1983
> 112–128

– fight against Maxwell in 1984
> 137–146

– retirement of
> 155

– biographical notes
> 81

Weavers, Frank
> 121, 123

Web Offset Conference
> 150

INDEX

Westall, Bernard
  89, 91–92
Whitehill, Cliff
  82
Whitelaw, David
  27
Whitten, Robin
  142
Willett, George
  142
Wills Tobacco Company
  22, 23, 24, 77
Wilson Barrett (actor manager)
  7, 38, 48
Winning Moves
  93
Woodhouse Moor
  3, 5, 42, 63
Woolworths
  26, 128
Worshipful Company of Makers
  of Playing Cards, the
  198, 131

York
  2, 12, 124, 198
Yorkshire
  1, 16, 64, 91, 118, 154, 198
Yorkshire County Cricket Club
  6
Yorkshire Evening Post, the
  180
Yorkshire Forward
  vii
Yorkshire Harlequin
  7
Yorkshire Post, the
  116, 159
Young, Martin (Company Secretary)
  v, 157, 163

ABOUT THE AUTHOR

VICTOR WATSON WAS born in Leeds in September 1928. He attended the Froebelian School in Horsforth and then Moorlands in Leeds, a school which was evacuated to Grasmere for two years during the war. He spent four years at Bootham School in York and then two years on National Service, during which he joined the Royal Engineers (Survey Unit) and reached the rank of 2nd Lieutenant. From there, he went on to Clare College Cambridge, where he read Natural Sciences for three years. In some of the gaps in all this he worked at Waddingtons. His practical experience and scientific education were important in the printing trade where he soon became completely absorbed by the work at Waddingtons.

As a sportsman he was adequate; enough said. As a pianist he could play well enough to amuse himself and enjoy the singing of comic songs.

Victor has served on the boards of eight companies other than Waddingtons. He served as President of the Royal Warrant Holders Association, the Printers Charitable Corporation, the Institute of Packaging; the British Printing Industries Federation and the Leeds Chamber of Commerce. He is a past Master of the Worshipful Company of Makers of Playing Cards.

He has helped Gateways School for girls, Bootham School, Martin House Hospice for Children, the Leeds International Pianoforte Competition, West Riding Opera, and the Royal Armouries, to name but a few organisations.

He was awarded the CBE in 1987 and was High Sheriff of West Yorkshire in 1989, and has been a Deputy Lieutenant since 1991. He was awarded Honorary Degrees by the University of Leeds and the Leeds Metropolitan University. He is a member of Alwoodley Golf Club. At Moortown Golf Club he has been Captain, Chairman and President.

He has a loyal wife and family and is proud of his two daughters and five grandchildren.